KU-687-477

The Internet in Public Life

EDITED BY VERNA V. GEHRING

ROWMAN & LITTLEFIELD PUBLISHERS, INC.
Lanham • Boulder • New York • Toronto • Oxford

LEEDS METROPOLITAN
UNIVERSITY
LIBRARY

1704331165
KV-B
CC-64543
10/6/05   14/7/05
303.483 INT

ROWMAN & LITTLEFIELD PUBLISHERS, INC.

Published in the United States of America
by Rowman & Littlefield Publishers, Inc.
A wholly owned subsidary of The Rowman & Littlefield Publishing Group, Inc.
4501 Forbes Boulevard, Suite 200, Lanham, Maryland 20706
www.rowmanlittlefield.com

PO Box 317
Oxford
OX2 9RU, UK

Copyright © 2004 by Rowman & Littlefield Publishers, Inc.

All rights reserved. No part of this publication may be reproduced,
stored in a retrieval system, or transmitted in any form or by any
means, electronic, mechanical, photocopying, recording, or otherwise,
without the prior permission of the publisher.

British Library Cataloguing in Publication Information Available

Library of Congress Cataloging-in-Publication Data

The Internet in public life / edited by Verna V. Gehring.
     p. cm. — (Institute for Philosophy and Public Policy studies)
  Includes bibliographical references and index.
  ISBN 0-7425-4233-5 (cloth : alk. paper) — ISBN 0-7425-4234-3 (pbk. : alk.
  paper)
     1. Internet—Social aspects. 2. Information society. 3. Social participation.
  4. Civil society. I. Gehring, Verna V. II. Series.

HM851.I582 2004
303.48'33—dc22   2004009862

Printed in the United States of America

⊗™ The paper used in this publication meets the minimum requirements of
American National Standard for Information Sciences—Permanence of Paper
for Printed Library Materials, ANSI/NISO Z39.48-1992.

The Internet in Public Life

LEEDS BECKETT UNIVERSITY
LIBRARY
DISCARDED

Leeds Metropolitan University

17 0433116 5

Institute for Philosophy & Public Policy Studies
General Editor: Verna V. Gehring

About the Series. This new series grows out of a collaboration between the Institute for Philosophy and Public Policy at the University of Maryland and Rowman & Littlefield Publishers. Each slim volume in the series offers an insightful, accessible collection of essays on a current topic of real public concern, and which lies at the intersection of philosophy and public policy. As such, these books are ideal resources for students and lay readers, while at the same time making a distinctive contribution to the broader scholarly discourse.

About the Institute. Established in 1976 at the University of Maryland and now part of the School of Public Affairs, the Institute for Philosophy and Public Policy was founded to conduct research into the conceptual and normative questions underlying public policy formation. This research is conducted cooperatively by philosophers, policy makers and analysts, and other experts both within and outside of government. The Institute publishes the journal *Philosophy & Public Policy Quarterly* and the series Institute for Philosophy and Public Policy Studies with Rowman & Littlefield Publishers.

Contents

II: Social Bonds: Stronger or Weaker?

Preface

Several of the essays in this work appeared as articles in *Philosophy & Public Policy Quarterly*, the journal sponsored by the Institute for Philosophy and Public Policy at the School of Public Affairs, University of Maryland. William A. Galston, director of the Institute for Philosophy and Public Policy, contributed the introduction, as well as one of the chapters, and research scholars of the Institute contributed three chapters. Peter Levine and Robert Wachbroit gratefully acknowledge funds from the Netherlands' School for Research in Practical Philosophy, and also Globus, Tilburg University's Institute for Globalization and Sustainable Development. This volume has benefited from the conversation and thought of all of the research scholars who offered suggestions for improvements to this volume. Thanks must go to Carroll Linkins and Richard Chapman for their help and kindness in bringing the essays to press.

The editor especially thanks William A. Galston, Peter Levine, and Robert Wachbroit for their helpful comments and thoughtful advice in the development of this volume.

Verna V. Gehring
Editor
Institute for Philosophy and Public Policy
School of Public Affairs, University of Maryland
College Park, Maryland

Introduction

William A. Galston

The spread of new information and communications technologies during the past two decades has helped reshape associations, political communities, and global relations. The speed of technology-driven change has outpaced our understanding of its social and ethical effects. This collection of essays, the third in the Institute for Philosophy and Public Policy Studies series, is designed to raise critical questions about these effects and to help catalyze a broader conversation.

Toward a Morality of Information?

The essays are divided into two groups. Authors in the first group explore, in different ways, the moral dimensions of the information revolution. Helen Nissenbaum and Lucas D. Introna argue the architecture of search engines has an important impact on access to, and the distribution of, information. If the design of search engines reflects only market imperatives, then existing asymmetries of wealth and power are bound to be reinforced. The Internet should be understood, at least in part, as a new form of public space and public good. As such, its design calls for democratic deliberation and collective decisions as well as disaggregated market choices.

Robert Wachbroit explores one of the defining and most celebrated features of the Internet—namely, its openness. He observes, as

have others, that this freedom comes at a price. Unlike newspapers
and traditional broadcast media, information on the Internet does not
typically pass through gatekeepers who try to assure its quality. The
result is a jumble of information, some highly reliable, some junk.
While search engines may impart a kind of order, they do little to
ensure reliability, or even to help users assess reliability. It is hard to
see how search engines could be redesigned to circumvent this problem, and proposals to institute net-appropriate information certifiers
raise new problems of their own. In the end, Wachbroit suggests, the
Internet calls for a special character-trait in its users: responsibility,
understood as the active assessment rather than passive acceptance of
net-based offerings. The more open the architecture of information,
the greater the costs of credulity.

Verna V. Gehring's essay extends the inquiry into the ethics of
information. She offers a double-barreled defense of "hackers" (not to
be confused with "crackers" and other information mavens who use
their technical skills for malign purposes). Not only do hackers serve
the public good—for example, by probing the flaws of security systems—but also they exemplify virtues our society needs: curiosity
and healthy skepticism; autonomy and responsibility; mutual aid and
public involvement; and even aesthetic subtlety.

Social Bonds: Stronger or Weaker?

In the second part of this collection, authors examine the effects of the
Internet on social bonds. My own contribution asks whether the
Internet helps build community. My answer is on the whole negative,
in part because the Internet does not appear to foster the kinds of relations among human beings that characterize community as ordinari-
ly understood, and also because the high level of individual choice
characteristic of Internet groups is likely to foster excessive fragmentation.

Peter Levine broadens and deepens the inquiry. In a wide-ranging
essay, he explores the impact of the Internet on social equity, social
connection, public deliberation, individual freedom, and personal privacy. His conclusion is that the technology itself does not determine
whether the Internet makes social bonds stronger and more richly satisfying, or flatter and weaker. The Internet will be what we choose to
make of it through democratic decisions, or, alternatively, what we
allow it to become through the operation of market forces. Like

Nissenbaum, he argues that we should tilt the current balance away from the market and back toward democracy.

Eric M. Uslaner uses survey data and sharp analysis to argue that the Internet neither builds nor destroys social capital. Trust and mistrust are stances toward the world that we develop elsewhere and then bring to the Internet. Moreover, he argues, Internet groups are not the kinds of communities that could generate social trust. The reason is straightforward: while the trust that holds societies together develops between peoples of differing backgrounds, Internet groups tend to be associations of individuals within common interests and shared views.

In the concluding chapter in this volume, Thomas C. Hilde extends the inquiry beyond the bounds of associations, communities, and even the nation-state. He asks whether the Internet can foster a kind of epistemic cosmopolitanism that could over time help build a more robust global community. His approach is cautiously optimistic: as he reads the evidence, the Internet helps develop a new kind of transnational civic activism, and technology-mediated links need not come at the expense of face-to-face communal bonds. Hilde concludes, as do several other contributors, that collective decisions yet to be made will prove crucial. In particular, the cosmopolitan potential of the Internet is more likely to be realized if nations choose to be guided by the findings and recommendations of the United Nations World Summit on the Information Society.

One thing seems clear: we are still at the early stage of social developments that will unfold over the next few decades. Previous transformative technologies—electricity, the automobile, radio and television, to name but a few—have defied the predictive capacities, not only of woolly-headed enthusiasts, but also of the sober scholars of their time. In retrospect, we can see that the outcomes reflected not only new technological possibilities, but also social choices driven by enduring human concerns. This combination will shape the future of information technology as well, whatever surprises its development may have in store.

The Information Superhighway: Toward a Morality of Information?

I

Shaping the Web: Why the Politics of Search Engines Matter

Helen Nissenbaum and Lucas D. Introna

The Internet, no longer merely an e-mail and file-sharing system, has emerged as a dominant interactive medium. Enhanced by the technology of the World Wide Web, the Internet is an integral part of the ever-expanding global media system, moving to the center stage of media politics alongside the traditional broadcast media of television and radio. Enthusiasts of the "new medium" herald the Internet as a democratizing force that will give voice to diverse social, economic, and cultural groups. It promises to give those who are traditionally disempowered access to typically unreachable nodes of power and previously inaccessible troves of information. To scholars of traditional media, these optimistic claims must have a ring of familiarity, echoing similar optimistic predictions concerning the democratizing and empowering capacities of both radio and television. Yet, as acclaimed media critic Robert McChesney and others have convincingly argued, commercial interests have been woven into the very fiber of the modern media networks, displacing and silencing the public service aspects central to the vision of the early pioneers of radio and television, and influencing such later innovations as media available via satellite and cable.

One finds divergent predictions on the prospects of the Internet. Some, such as information policy expert Dan Schiller, along with McChesney, anticipate a narrowing of prospects for the Internet, pointing to the US's commitment to private ownership of communications technology as a consistent historical policy position. Others, like Mark Poster, offer a contrasting view, arguing that the distinctly "postmodern" nature of the Internet, with its capacity to disseminate material rather than centralize it, discourages the aggregation of authority. The Internet, according to this view, is unlikely to mirror the development of previous media.

The debate about the possibilities of media either to be democratized in the service of the public good, or to be colonized by specialized interests, motivates this article on the politics of search engines. The general position we defend is that, despite the prospects of the Internet and the Web for furthering the public good, their benefits are conditional, resting precariously on a number of political, economic, and technical factors. Following Mark Poster, we are encouraged by clear instances in which the Web and the Internet have served broad political ends. But, like McChesney, we also see irrefutable signs of gradual centralization and commercialization of guiding forces. We are particularly concerned with the way the competing interests of centralized commercial interests versus decentralized public interests may be woven in, or out of, the very fiber of media networks. Search engines constitute a powerful source of access and accessibility within the Web. Access to information on the Web is the subject of much scholarship and research. In a statistical study of Web search engines, S. Lawrence and C. L. Giles estimated that none of the search engines they studied, taken individually, index more than 16 percent of the total indexable Web, which they estimate to consist of 800 million pages. Combining the results of the search engines they studied, they estimated coverage to increase to approximately 42 percent. One must remain mindful, however, that a sizeable portion of the Web will remain hidden from view. Developers, designers, and producers of search engines confront technological limitations that at present determine systematic inclusions and exclusions, dictating prominence for some sites and invisibility for others. We examine these technological challenges, and contend that they pose political challenges as well, since what people (the "seekers") are able to find on the Web determines the possibilities—and limitations—of what they can gain information about and with whom they can communicate.

Following a brief discussion of how search engines work and how they can—but might not—make finding particular Web pages easy or even possible, we discuss the proposition that market influences introduce innovations in search engine technology, and better access to information available on the Web. We conclude that the Web must be viewed as a public good and future development must include political discussion and public policy considerations.

A Brief and Selective Technical Overview

Anyone who wants to make sure his or her Web page can be successfully accessed by others must seek recognition from search engines for their Web pages, which focuses on two key tasks: (1) being indexed, and (2) achieving a ranking in the top 10–20 search results displayed.

On Being Indexed. Without much exaggeration one could say that to exist is to be indexed by a search engine. If a Web page is not in the index of a search engine, the person seeking access must know the complete URL—Web page address—such as http://www. rowmanlittlefield.com/—in this case, the Rowman & Littlefield Web site, the site of the publisher of this book. There exists no rigid standard for producing URLs; addresses are not obvious or even logical in the way we tend to think that the addresses of our physical homes are logical. Sometimes the Internet domain name structure may help, such as "edu" for an academic institution. However, for most searches, one could not reasonably guess at a URL.

This is where search engines enter the picture. They first create a map of the Web by indexing Web pages according to keywords, and then create enormous databases that link page content, to keywords, to URLs. When a seeker of information submits a keyword (or phrase)—presumably, one that best captures her interest—the search engine database can return to the seeker a list of URLs linked to that keyword and, ideally, relevant to the seeker's interest. Notably, search engines use the notion of a keyword (i.e., that which is indexed and hence used for searching) in a rather minimal sense. Keywords are not determined by the designers of the search engines' databases; rather, they are "deduced" from those Web pages being indexed. Clearly, it is important for Web page producers as well as seekers to know what words on a particular Web page are "seen" as keywords by the indexing software of search engines.

Directory-based search engines. Search engines can create their databases and determine what to store in them in one of two ways. The pages indexed in directory-based search engines such as Yahoo! are manually submitted to the search engines' editors by Webmasters (and other creators of Web pages). Someone wanting her page recognized by Yahoo!, for example, would submit the URL and background information to a human editor who reviews the page(s) and decides whether or not to schedule her page for indexing. Pages accepted for indexing are retrieved by the indexing software that then index them according to the keywords (content) found in the page. Human gatekeepers determine inclusion in their indexed databases, and there can exist a backlog of up to six months from the time of submission to the time of inclusion.

The criteria human editors use in deciding whether to accept a page for indexing can be vague. Representatives of Yahoo!, for example, report that they use criteria of relevancy, but the exact nature of these criteria is not widely known, not publicly disseminated, and, evidently, not consistently applied by the various editors. As a result, someone might have his page rejected (with no notification), and without knowing what to do to gain acceptance. Danny Sullivan, the editor of *Search Engine Watch,* believes that the base success rate for a page submitted to Yahoo! is approximately 25 percent. Two factors that seem to increase the chances of being listed are the number of links (to and from a given site—also referred to as inlinks and outlinks), and how full a particular category happens to be (since, when editors feel they need more references within a category, they lower the entry barriers). Defending their approach, representatives of Yahoo! maintain that they list what users want, arguing that if users were not finding relevant information they would cease using Yahoo!. (We will return to this form of response below.)

Spider-based search engines. Search engines such as Google, Alta Vista, Lycos, and Hotbot, by contrast, rely on "spiders" as an alternative method. Spiders (also called robots, crawlers, softbots, and agents, among other terms) usually start crawling from a historical list of URLs, especially documents with many links elsewhere, such as server lists, "What's New" pages, and other popular sites on the Web. Software robots automatically traverse the Web's hypertext structure—first retrieving a document, and then recursively retrieving all documents that are linked by other URLs in the original document. Web owners interested in having their pages indexed might wish they had access to the detail of routes that robots follow when they crawl, which sites they favor, which ones they visit and how often, which not, and so forth. But these matters are steadfastly guarded trade secrets by search engine companies.

But one can make reasonable inferences about the character of search engine crawl algorithms. Among useful discussions of efficient crawling are those by researchers Junghoo Cho and Hector Garcia-Molina, working with Google cofounder Larry Page, who disclose some of the metrics spiders use to determine the "importance" of a Web page. They identify four crucial criteria on which algorithms are based.

Given any Web page, P, one can define the importance of that page, I (P), in one of the following ways:

1. Similarity to a Driving Query Q. *A query Q drives the crawling process,* and I(P) is defined to be the *textual similarity* between P and Q.

2. Backlink Count. The value of I(P) is *the number of links to P that appear over the entire Web, IB(P). Intuitively, a page P that is linked to by many pages is more important than one that is seldom referenced.* Evaluating IB(P) requires counting backlinks over the entire Web; a crawler can estimate this value with IB'(P), the number of links to P that have been seen so far.

3. Page Rank. The IB(P) metric treats all links equally. Thus, a link from the Yahoo! home page counts the same as a link from some individual's home page. However, since the Yahoo! home page is more important (it has a much higher IB count), it makes sense to value that link more highly. *The page rank backlink metric, IR(P), recursively defines the importance of a page to be the weighted sum of the backlinks to it.* Such a metric has been found to be very useful in ranking results of user queries. IR'(P) is used to estimate the value of IR(P) when only a subset of pages is available.

4. Location Metric. The IL(P) importance of page P is a function of its location, not of its contents. If URL u leads to P, then IL(P) is a function of u. For example, URLs ending with ".com" may be deemed more useful than URLs with other endings. Another location metric that is sometimes used considers URLs with fewer slashes more useful than those with more slashes. This metric is local, since it can be evaluated simply by looking at the URLs.

Each of these metrics is problematic. The "similarity to a driving query Q" metric uses a query term or string (Q)—such as "holiday cottages," for example—as the basic heuristic for crawling. The spider does not need to make a decision about "importance" since it is directed in its search by the query string itself. For our discussion, this metric is of minor significance. The real issue emerges when the crawling spider must "decide" importance without the use of a sub-mitted query term. This is where the other metrics play the dominant role.

The backlink metric uses the backlink (or inlink) count as its "importance" heuristic, applying the reasonable insight that a page linked to many other pages is more important than one that is seldom referenced. Academic research stresses a similar insight, counseling the wisdom of looking at the "canonical" works frequently cited by other authors. But not all topics necessarily have canons, and in some fields, many citations are needed to reach canonical status. Thus, the backlink heuristic tends to gather the large topics or fields (such as "shareware computer games") since an even relatively unimportant site in this big field will be seen as more "important"—have relative-ly more backlinks or inlinks—than a truly important site in a small field (such as "the local community services information" page), with fewer backlinks or inlinks. The essential point is that large fields determine the measure of "importance" *through sheer volume of back-links* in ways that tend to eliminate equally important small fields.

The page rank metric exacerbates this problem, since rather than treating all links equally, this heuristic gives prominence to backlinks from other "important" pages—pages with high backlink counts. Both backlink and page rank metrics can be manipulated by, for instance, inducing Web page creators to add a link to their page through incentives such as discounts on products, free software utili-ties, and access to exclusive information.

The location metric uses location information from the URL as the basis of decision making, and one can rely on a variety of elements to catch the attention of the crawling spider, such as possession of the right domain name, or location in the root directory. Pages with many backlinks, especially backlinks from other pages with high backlink counts, which reside in locations seen as "useful" or "important" to the crawling spider, become targets for harvesting.

A final consideration is whether a spider is guided by breadth or depth of representation. The spider favoring breadth over depth vis-its more sites (or hosts) and indexes these only partially. In the case of big sites such as America On Line (AOL) or Geocities, spiders index at a rate of approximately 10–15 percent, and thus creators of sites hosted by AOL or another big site likely will find that their site is excluded from indexing.

On Ranking

Indexing is bu'   'o clear for the creators of Web pages who
strive for r   ndexed, the concern shifts to ranking.
Many o'   1 by a person doing a search, a Web
page   p ten to twenty "hits." A study of
t^   ' airline reservations systems
          t agents selected a flight from
          ^uggestive of what we might
          ^igners jealously compete
          ^ site promotion report

          ` day. They are
          ^ and learn the
          ^ ways to "bump
          ^n sites.

          ^le empirical studies meas-
ur^   ^iavior of seekers, we observe
anec^   ^o look down a list and then cease
looking

Besid^   ^nallenges, experts in relevancy ranking
must strugg.   ^illenge of approximating a complex human
value ("releva.   ^th a computer algorithm. According to these
experts, while w^ ^eem to be mastering the coverage issue, we continue to struggle with the issue of what precisely to extract from the
enormous bulk of possibilities for a given search.

Most ranking algorithms of search engines use both the position
and the frequency of keywords as a basis for their ranking heuristics.
Accordingly, a document with high frequency of keywords in the
beginning of a document is seen as more relevant (relative to the keyword entered) than one with low frequency lower down in the document. Other ranking schemes, like that used by Lycos, are based on
so-called "in-link" popularity. The popularity score for a particular
site is calculated from the total number of other sites that contain links
to that site. As with the crawl metrics discussed above, one sees the
standard or threshold of "relevance" set by the big sites at the expense
of equally relevant small sites.

The battle for high ranking has generated a field of knowledge,
"search engine design," which teaches how to design a Web page in
order to optimize its ranking and combines these teachings with soft-

The Civic Quarter Library
www.leedsmet.ac.uk/lis/lss

Borrowed Customer
Elbeskri, Fauzia (Mrs)

1 The internet in pu
1704331165

17/10/2011,23:59
Due Date

For renewals telephone (0113) 812 6161
Thank you and see you soon
03.10.2011 14:47:51

ware to assess its ranking potential. On the one end of the spectrum, practices that make use of reasonable heuristics help designers optimize their Web pages' expected rankings. But on the other end of the spectrum, some schemes allow Web designers to manipulate rankings by, for instance, tricking the ranking algorithm into giving a higher ranking by such means as keyword stuffing, or using invisible text or tiny text. This dubious art of manipulation has become known as relevancy (or keyword) spamming. Out of this strange ranking warfare has emerged an impossible situation: search engine operators are loath to disclose details of their ranking algorithms for fear that spammers will use this knowledge to trick them. Yet ethical Web page designers legitimately defend their need to know how to design for, or indicate relevancy to, the ranking algorithm, arguing that seekers are entitled to find what is genuinely relevant to their searches.

Besides second-guessing ranking algorithms, some producers of Web sites elevate their rankings by a nontechnical approach: They try to buy a high ranking. This subject is an especially sensitive one, and representatives of several major search engines indignantly deny that they sell search positions. Recently, however, in a much-publicized move, Alta Vista and Doublclick have invited advertisers to bid for position in their top slots. Yahoo! sells prominence indirectly by allowing Web owners to pay for express indexing. This allows them to move ahead in the six-month queue. Another method for buying prominence—less controversial but not unproblematic—allows Web owners to buy keywords for purposes of banner ads. Amazon Books, for example, has a comprehensive arrangement with Yahoo! If a seeker submits a search to Yahoo! with the term "book" in it, or a term with a name that corresponds to an author's name or book title in the Amazon database, he would get the Amazon banner (and URL) on his or her search result screen. This is also true for many other companies and products. The battle for ranking is fought not only between search engines and Webmasters or designers but also among organizations themselves. One finds sufficient evidence suggesting that fierce competition for both presence and prominence has led to such nefarious practices as one organization retrieving a competitor's Web page, editing it so that it would not rank well, and resubmitting it as an updated submission. In another case, an organization bought a competitor's name as a keyword so that the first organization's banner and URL are displayed when a keyword search is done on the competitor's name.

Based on these findings of how search engines work, we would predict that information seekers are *most likely* to find those sites constructed by designers with the technical savvy to succeed in the ranking game, and whose proprietors pay to improve their site's positioning. Seekers are *less likely* to find less popular, smaller sites, including those that are not supported by knowledgeable professionals. When a search does yield these sites, they typically have lower rankings. These predictions are, of course, highly general and vary considerably according to the keywords or phrases used by seekers, and a seeker's own competence. Some users actively seek one search engine over others, but some will simply, and perhaps unknowingly, use a default engine provided by institutions or Internet service providers (ISPs).

Should the Market Decide?

Some might not be troubled by the ways search engines produce results, contending that one ought to let producers of search engines do what they will and let users decide freely which they like best. Search engines whose offerings are skewed, so the argument goes, will suffer in the marketplace. As the representatives of Yahoo! have argued, users' reactions must remain the benchmark of quality. Dissatisfied seekers will defect from an inadequate search engine to others that do a better job. The best search engines flourish, while the poor ones will fade away from lack of use. Robert McChesney describes a comparable faith in the market mechanism as it applies to traditional broadcast media:

> In the United States, the notion that commercial broadcasting is the superior system because it embodies market principles is closely attached to the notion that the market is the only "democratic" regulatory mechanism, and that this democratic market is the essence of Americanism, patriotism, and all that is good and true in the world.

Both McChesney and Schiller, among others, have criticized the idea that a media market best represents democratic ideals. In the case of search engines, we are, likewise, not optimistic about the promise of development shaped only by a marketplace. The dominant search engines do not charge seekers for the search service. Rather, just as commercial television advertisers pay television stations in hopes of gaining access to viewers, search engines attract paid advertisements based on the promise of search usage. High usage, presumably, garners advertisers and high charges. To succeed, therefore, search engines must establish a reputation for satisfying seekers' desires and needs.

One might pointedly ask on what grounds one would presume to override the wishes of users so cleanly reflected in their market choices? Our reply reflects two concerns: One is that the conditions needed for a marketplace to function in a "democratic" and efficient way are simply not met in the case of search engines. The other is our judgment that Web search mechanisms are too important to be shaped by the marketplace alone. We discuss each in turn.

Marketplace Conditions and the Internet

Defenders of the market mechanism frequently claim that participants can freely express their preferences through choices made among alternatives. Incompetent and inefficient suppliers are eliminated in favor of competent, efficient ones. But this scenario holds true only in markets where suppliers of goods or services have an equal possibility to enter the market and communicate with potential customers, and where potential purchasers are fully informed and can act rationally. Such a market simply does not exist in the case of search engines.

Most users of the Web lack critical information about alternatives. Only a fraction understand how search engines work and how results are generated. It is misleading to suggest that users meaningfully express preferences or exercise free choice when they select from the alternatives. Further, users tend to be ignorant about the inherent partiality present in any search engine search results (discussed in the technical overview above). Most users tend to treat search engine results the way they treat library catalogue search results. Given the vastness of the Web, the close guarding of algorithms, and the abstruseness of the technology to most users, it should come as no surprise that seekers are unfamiliar, even unaware, of the systematic mechanisms that drive search engines. Such awareness, we believe, would make a difference. When customers learned that Amazon Books, for example, had been representing as "friendly" recommendations what were in reality paid advertisements, customers responded with great ire and Amazon hastily retreated.

The problem is equally complex on the supply side of the market. Complex hurdles must be cleared to be listed and ranked appropriately. These obstacles are evidence that the playing field is not level, and thus the "market will decide" view is extremely problematic in this context.

The question of whether a marketplace in search engines approximates a competitive free market is, perhaps, subordinate to the question of whether search mechanisms *ought* to be shaped by the marketplace to begin with.

Two distinct forces shape developments in Web searching. The collective preferences of seekers drive search engine designers to try to achieve greatest popularity by catering to majority interests. But popularity with seekers is not the only force at play. There also exists the force exerted by entities wishing to be found. Here, there is enormous inequality. Some enter the market already wielding vastly greater prowess and economic power than others. The rich and powerful clearly can influence the tendencies of search engines; their dollars play a decisive a role in what gets "found." For example, of the top 100 sites—based on traffic—just six are not ".com" commercial sites. If we exclude universities, NASA, and the US government, this drops to two. One could reasonably argue that the United Nations site ought to generate at least enough traffic to be in the list if we consider that Amazon is in position number 10 and *USA Today* in position 35. The cost to a search engine of losing a small number of searching customers may be outweighed by the benefits of pandering to "the masses" and to entities paying fees for the various forms of enhanced visibility. We can expect, therefore, that at least some drift will be caused by those wishing to be found which, in turn, would further narrow the field of what is available to seekers of information, association, support, and services.

One can think of the Web as a market of markets instead of as just one market. Seekers are not interested in "information" in general; they want specific information related to specific interests and needs. Those seeking information about, for example, "packaged tour holidays" or "computer hardware suppliers" are approached by companies competing for recognition. Some of these companies might pay high prices for keyword banners that ensure them top rankings. By contrast, significantly smaller markets—for information about a rare medical condition, or about services of a local government authority or community—would face little, if any, competition.

In this market of markets, there might be little incentive to ensure inclusion for these small markets, and only a small cost (in loss of participation) results from their exclusion. One could imagine that a high percentage of search requests (say 80 percent, for argument's sake) are directed to a small percentage (say 20 percent) of the big markets, which would be abundantly represented in search results. Only a small percentage of the search requests (say 20 percent) might be addressed to the large percentage (say 80 percent) of the smaller markets, which would be underrepresented. This scenario explains the limited incentive for inclusion and relatively low cost of exclusion. This consequence is problematic.

Although a market enthusiast is not troubled by this result, one can reasonably maintain that the variety of options on the Web is of special importance. The value of comprehensive, thorough, and wide-ranging access to the Web lies within the category of goods that Elizabeth Anderson describes in her book, *Values in Ethics and Economics* as goods that should not be left entirely (if at all) to the marketplace.

As part of her extended argument that one must place ethical limitations on the scope of market norms for a range of goods (and services), Anderson convincingly contends that certain goods—ones that she calls "political goods," including among them schools and public places—should be distributed not according to market norms but "in accordance with public principles" that express the values of a liberal democratic society like ours, which is committed to "freedom, autonomy, and welfare."

Sustaining the 80 percent of small markets that would be neglected by search engines shaped by market forces qualifies as a task worthy of public attention. Societies make political decisions to "save" certain goods that might fall by the wayside in a purely market-driven society. Public policy recognizes and saves national treasures, historic homes, public parks, and schools; it serves disadvantaged groups, such as the disabled, even though (and because) a market mechanism does not cater to their needs; it makes special accommodation for non-profit efforts through tax-exemption without consideration for popularity. One can make the case that there exists an equivalent need in the case of search engines. Search engines are a special, political good that must be designed and used well in order to take full advantage of the Web, which also is a special good.

The Future of the Web as a Public Good

Search engines raise political concerns not simply because of the way they function, but also because the way they function is at odds with the view of the Web as a public good. Over the course of the past decade computerized networks—the Internet and now the Web— have increasingly been envisioned as a great public good. This view is based on past achievements and also on future promises. For example, with only a fraction of the US population linked to the Internet, in 1995 then vice president Al Gore promoted the vision of a Global Internet Infrastructure. This conception of the great public good— part reality, part wishful thinking—has gripped people from a variety of sectors, including scholars, engineers and scientists, entrepreneurs and politicians. Each has highlighted a particular dimension of the Web's promise, some focusing on information, some on communication, some on commerce, and so on.

One theme woven through most versions of the promise of the Web hails its power to promote public good by serving as a special kind of public space. The Web seems to be public in the sense that its hardware and software infrastructure is not wholly owned by any person or institution, or, for that matter, by any single nation. Arguably, it does not fall under the territorial jurisdiction of any existing sovereign state. There is no central clearinghouse that specifies or vets content, or regulates the right of access. All those who accept technical protocols, conform to technical standards (HTML, for example) and are able to connect to it, may "enter" the Web. The collaborative nature of activity on the Web leads to a sense that the Web is not simply unowned but is collectively owned.

The Web also fulfills some of the functions of other traditional public spaces—museums, parks, beaches, and schools. It is a medium for artistic expression, a space for recreation, a place for storing and exhibiting items of historical and cultural importance. It is hailed as a medium for intensive communication. It is the Hyde Park Corner of the electronic age, the public square where people may gather as a whole, or associate in smaller groups. They may talk and listen, plan and organize, air viewpoints and deliberate. Such spaces, where content is regulated by only a few fundamental rules, embody the ideals of the liberal democratic society.

The idea of the Web as a public space and a forum for political deliberation has fueled numerous discussions on "teledemocracy." The notion of the public sphere as a forum in which communicatively rational dialogue can take place unsullied by ideology has had one of its strongest proponents in the philosopher Jürgen Habermas. Although one finds no universal agreement among scholars on the extent to which the Web influences the political sphere, scholars agree that the Web appears to have played a crucial role in such political events as the Zapatista struggle against the Mexican government, the Tiananmen Square democracy movement, environmental activists who exposed McDonald's through the McLibel campaign, and the Clean Clothes Campaign supporting attempts of Filipino garment workers to expose exploitative working conditions.

Perhaps the most compelling reason to conceive of the Web as a public good is because it effectively stores and conveys information. It increasingly is a repository for many types of information—government documents, consumer goods, scientific and artistic works, and local public announcements, to name a few. Further, in this so-called "information age," being among the information-rich is considered so important that some, such as the philosopher Jeroen van den Hoven, argue that access to information is one of the "primary goods," to which the political philosopher John Rawls insists that, to be considered just, a society must guarantee that access to all citizens. The Web should not further expand the gap between haves and have-nots; rather, it should narrow that gap.

The view of the Internet as a public good fueled much of the initial social and economic investment in it and its supporting technology. The vision motivated idealistic computer scientists and engineers to volunteer their energy and expertise. Among them, Jonathan Postel, one of the early builders of the Internet, worked to keep its standards open and free, and numerous experts helped wire schools and build infrastructure. These inclusive values were very much in the minds of creators of the Web, such as Tim Berners-Lee:

> The universality of the Web includes the fact that the information space can represent anything from one's personal private jottings to a polished global publication. We as people can, with or without the Web, interact on all scales. By being involved on every level, we ourselves form the ties which weave the levels together into a sort of consistency, balancing the homogeneity and the heterogeneity, the harmony and the diversity. We can be involved on a personal, family, town, corporate, state, national, union, and international levels. Culture exists at all levels, and we should give it a weighted, balanced respect at each level.

While the promise of the Web as a public space and a public good continues to galvanize general, political, and commercial support, many observers and scholars advise caution. The benefits of the vast

Information Policy Conference, Vancouver, October 27–28, 1995; Mark Poster, "CyberDemocracy: Internet and the Public Sphere, " in *Internet Culture*, edited by David Porter (New York: Routledge, 1995). For scholarly discussions on search engines as a powerful source of access and accessibility within the Web, see, for instance: Peter Golding, "The Communications Paradox: Inequality at the National and International Levels," *Media Development*, vol. 4 (1994); Donna L. Hoffman and Thomas P. Novak, "Bridging the Racial Divide on the Internet," *Science*, vol. 280 (1998); Andrew Pollack, "A Cyberspace Front in a Multicultural War," *New York Times* (August 7, 1995) and also coauthored with A. Hockley, "What's Wrong with Internet Searching?" *D-Lib Magazine* (March 1997). Also, a lengthy report of the National Telecommunications and Information Administration (NTIA), "Falling through the Net," finds that access to the Web is preconfigured in subtle but politically important ways. S. Lawrence and C. L. Giles, "Accessibility and Distribution of Information on the Web," *Nature*, vol. 400 (1999). Keywords are deduced from those Web pages being indexed; for instance, in a particular Web page a keyword(s) can be actual keywords indicated by the Web page designer (in an HTML metatag as follows: <meta NAME="keywords" CONTENT="list of keywords">); all, or some of the words appearing in the title of the page (indicated by the HTML <TITLE> tag as <TITLE>); the first X words in a Web page; or even all of the words in the Web page. The Yahoo! criteria of relevancy are discussed in V. Phua, *Towards a Set of Ethical Rules for Search Engines*, MSc dissertation, London School of Economics, 1998; J. Cho, H. Garcia-Molina, and L. Page, "Efficient Crawling through URL Ordering," Seventh International World Wide Web Conference, Brisbane, Australia, April 14–18, 1998. For the study of travel agents using computerized airline reservation systems, see B. Friedman and H. Nissenbaum, "Bias in Computer Systems," *ACM Transactions on Information Systems*, vol. 14 (1996); the quote that "people are trying to take away top spots every day . . . " occurs in Patrick Anderson and Michael Henderson, "Hits To Sales," (1997) http://www.hitstosales.com/2search.html; on ranking algorithms of search engines using both the position and the frequency of keywords as a basis for their ranking heuristics, see G. Pringle, L. Allison, and D. L. Dowe, "What Is a Tall Poppy among Webpages?" Seventh International World Wide Web Conference, Brisbane, Australia, April 14–18, 1998 http://www7.scu.edu.au/programme/fullpapers/1872/com1872.htm; S. Hansell, "Altavista Invites Advertisers to Pay for Top Ranking," *New York Times* (April 15, 1999); Robert W. McChesney, *Corporate Media and the Threat to Democracy* (New York: Seven Stories Press, 1997); Elizabeth Anderson, *Value in Ethics and Economics* (Cambridge and London: Harvard University Press, 1993); for useful discussions concerning teledemocracy, see: Jeffrey B. Abramson, F. C. Arterton, and G. R. Orren, *The Electronic Commonwealth: The Impact of New Media Technologies on Democratic Politics* (New York: Basic Books, 1988), and F. Christopher Arterton, *Teledemocracy: Can Technology Protect Democracy?* (Newbury Park, CA: Sage, 1987). Jürgen Habermas, *The Structural Transformation of the Public Sphere,* translated by T. Burger and F. Lawrence (Cambridge, MA: Harvard University Press, 1989). On the Web's role in political events, see Douglas Kellner, "Intellectuals, the New Public Spheres, and Techno-Politics," 1997, available at: http://www.gseis.ucla.edu/courses/ed253a/newDK/intell.htm; Jeroen van den Hoven, "Towards Ethical Principles for Designing Politico-Administrative Information Systems, " *Informatization in the Public Sector,* vol. 3 (1994); for further discussion of the point John Rawls makes, that society must guarantee access to all citizens, specifically that the Web should not further expand the gap between have and have-nots, see Richard Civille, "The Internet and the Poor," in *Public Access to the Internet,* edited by Brian Kahin and James Keller (Cambridge, MA: MIT Press, 1996) and the Hoffman and Novak article. Tim Berners-Lee, *Weaving the Web: The Original Design and Ultimate Destiny of the World Wide Web by its Inventor,* with coauthors Mark Fischetti and Michael Dertouzos (San Francisco: Harper, 1999); Lewis Branscomb, "Balancing the Commercial and Public-Interest Visions," in *Public Access to the Internet,* edited by Brian Kahin and James Keller (Cambridge, MA: MIT Press, 1996); on standardized methods for Internet equivalents for the White and Yellow Page directories, see: Marvin Sirbu, "Telecommunications Technology and Infrastructure," in *A National Information Network: Changing Our Lives in the 21st Century* (Nashville, TN and Queenstown, MD: Institute for Information Studies, 1992); Marc Raboy, "Global Communication Policy and Human Rights, " in *A Communications Cornucopia: Markle Foundation Essays on Information Policy,* edited by Roger G. Noll and Monroe E. Price (Washington, DC: Brookings Institution Press, 1998); Amartya Sen, *On Ethics and Economics* (Oxford: Blackwell, 1987) and also see his "The Moral Standing of the Market," *Social Philosophy & Policy,* vol. 2 (1985); on existing asymmetries of power, see Robert W. McChesney, "The Mythology of Commercial Media and the Contemporary Crisis of Public Broadcasting," Spry Memorial Lecture (Montreal & Vancouver, December 2 and 4, 1997) and also Robert W. McChesney and Edward S. Herman, *The Global Media: The New Missionaries of Corporate Capitalism* (London: Cassell, 1997); for further discussion that technological systems embody values resonating in social and political commentary, see Lawrence Lessig, *Code and Other Laws of Cyberspace* (New York: Basic Books, 1999) and Helen Nissenbaum, "Values in the Design of Computer Systems," *Computers in Society*

(March 1998); on the notion of individualized robots searching for pages based on individual criteria, see Martijn Kostner, "Robots in the web: threat or treat, " found at: http://info.webcrawler.com; on improvement on the way individual pages indicate relevance, see: M. Marchiori, "The Limits of Web Metadata, and Beyond," Seventh International World Wide Web Conference, Brisbane, Brisbane, Australia, April 14–18, 1998. http://www7.scu.edu.au/programme/fullpapers/1896/com1896.htm. On improvements to Web resource presentation see Marti Hearst, "Interfaces for searching the Web," *Scientific American* (March, 1997) and found at http://www.sciam.com/0397issue/039/hearst.html; further discussion of metasearch technology can be found at: S. Lawrence and C. L. Giles, "Inquirus, the NECI meta search engine," delivered at the Seventh International World Wide Web Conference, Brisbane, Australia, April 14–18, 1998 and available at: http://www7.scu.edu.au/programme/fullpapers/1906/com1906.htm.

Reliance and Reliability: The Problem of Information on the Internet

Robert Wachbroit

Internet use has grown astonishingly in the past few years. With little effort one can learn what legislation is pending in Congress, the status of medical research in various universities and institutes, and the biographies of both the famous and the obscure. The Internet also offers countless sources of news—from traditional sources, such as the *New York Times* and CNN, to more partisan but sometimes more probing advocacy groups. For information junkies, there is little that can beat the Internet. The good news is that everything is on the Internet. The bad news is that everything is on the Internet.

In all likelihood, future use of the Internet will only increase and, as it does, some of us will rely on the Internet for much—perhaps all—of our information. Not all of this information will be reliable. But even if much of it is, heavy reliance on the Internet for information may present a worry. This essay examines the problems of information reliability and reliance on the Internet and looks at some of the difficulties raised by recent attempts to address these problems.

The Problem of Reliability

As many people have noted, anyone with access to the Internet can be a publisher. If you can write it down, you can put it up on the Web for millions to read. As a result, the Internet is an enormous source of information and an enormous source of misinformation. One can easily come across rumors, gossip, ideological rantings, paranoid accusations, lunatic ravings, outright lies, and wishful thinking—all just a mouse-click away from the more reliable information on the Internet.

Is this so significant? After all, rumors, gossip, and so on, have always been with us. We shouldn't be at all surprised that misinformation has a future in every advance of telecommunications technology. Soon after the invention of the telephone, the word "phony" entered the American language. The word, referring to a fake or a counterfeit, apparently arose from the increasingly common experience, by the beginning of the twentieth century, that the friendly voice on the telephone was too often the voice of a swindler. Today we have grown appropriately cautious about phone calls from strangers, realizing that the benefits of the technology allow for some abuses.

Nevertheless, the consequences of misinformation on the Internet can be significant. The Internet is much like a broadcast medium, spreading messages rapidly, widely, and effortlessly. But unlike most broadcast media, messages can be posted anonymously or with a pseudonym so that checking the source is difficult. At a single click, more people can be misled than is possible with the telephone. Consider some examples:

A teenager was charged with securities fraud, after apparently buying thinly traded stocks and then, using a number of pseudonyms, posting numerous messages on the Internet touting the stock. Those who believed that enthusiasm for the stock was growing bid up its price, which soon dropped once they realized that no such enthusiasm existed for the stock. But by that time, the teenager had sold his holdings at a profit.

The Internet is an increasingly important resource for those seeking information about medical conditions. But individuals searching for information on cancer can easily discover Dr. Ryke Geerd Hamer's Web site (www.geocities.com/HotSprings/3374/entdeck.htm), which claims to explain what cancer really is. Not only does the information on this site fall into the dangerous category of quack medicine—among other advice, the doctor urges people to abandon "official medical treatments"—but the site also fails to inform the reader that Dr. Hamer was arrested for illegally practicing medicine.

Not all the misinformation on the Web is expensive or dangerous, however. Some is just utter nonsense, as is the case of the Web site for the Oklahoma Association of Wine Producers (www.members.aol.com/okawp/). Those who are aware that Oklahoma has no wine industry might be amused by the site, but one can also imagine someone planning a tour of Oklahoma's wineries after reading the "information" on the site. (The authors of the site intend it as an educational tool regarding misinformation on the Internet, but one has to examine the site carefully to see the disclaimer.)

Intermediaries and Gatekeepers

Several writers see the problem of reliability as arising from the demise of "information intermediaries." In traditional information outlets—major newspapers and book publishers, most notably—several layers of intermediaries exist between the writer and the reader. These intermediaries ensure the correctness of what is written. The reader knows that, for example, the reputation of the *New York Times* is behind each of its stories and that the editors, production staff, managers, and legal counsel work hard to ensure that the reputation of the paper is well deserved. The reader can thus trust what he reads in the *New York Times* because of the information intermediaries it employs. But once these layers of intermediaries are removed, a mechanism for ensuring reliability is dismantled. As Andrew Shapiro notes, "Where once there were reporters, writers, editors, fact-checkers, production staff, publishers, libel lawyers, and large media owners, now a worldwide dispatch may be the result of a quirky thought and a bit of tapping at a keyboard in one's bedroom."

This explanation of the problem suggests an obvious response. If the reliability of these traditional sources of information is acceptable, then reliable Web sites could consist of these sources having an online presence. And indeed, many of them do. Nearly every major newspaper has a Web site where many of its articles are posted, and these sites are as reliable as their print counterparts. This practice is not confined to newspapers—many commercial, governmental, and nonprofit entities have also created an online presence.

One might respond, of course, that such efforts in no way eliminate or control the presence of unreliable Web sites. But that is not the issue. The concern is not the presence of unreliable Web sites—we will always have them, just as we have always had unreliable sources of information prior to the development of the Internet. The concern is identifying the reliable sources—distinguishing trustworthy information from fake. Having respectable sources maintain an online presence seems to ease this concern.

Unfortunately, this response doesn't go as far as it needs to. It undervalues the potential of the Internet, treating it merely as a new medium that happens to be inexpensive and easy. But what excites so many people about the Internet is not so much that it is cheap and convenient but rather that it is decentralized and open. Anyone can post information without facing censorship and without seeking the approval of some information gatekeeper. Some might say that the more controversial the information, the more important is the availability of the Internet. The Internet can be a powerful democratizing force, especially in repressive societies where information is tightly controlled. Even in more open societies, it is essential for democracy that the public can get information outside of the mainstream. Identifying reliable Web sites simply on the basis of a reliable offline presence excludes the important new sources of information that the Web can provide.

Rather than intermediaries ensuring accuracy, one might propose some sort of certification procedure. Reliable Web sites could display some seal which attests to their adherence to a set of standards regarding the quality of the information presented. For example, a Web site that describes the treatment options for a particular form of cancer might reassure readers of the trustworthiness of its information by displaying a seal of approval from, for instance, the National Institutes of Health or the American Medical Association.

Despite its initial promise, a certification procedure amounts to the reintroduction of information intermediaries—perhaps not at the level of introducing people who are fact-checkers and editors, but at a metalevel of experts who certify the practices and authority of a Web site. While this might enable some new sites to emerge as information sources, trust in the site's accuracy would actually reside in the site's certifiers. Further, a certification process would prove unhelpful when information is deemed controversial. In fact, one can easily imagine someone unfairly stigmatizing some sites as unreliable simply because they did not have the time, resources, or awareness to submit themselves to certification. Certification raises obvious questions, finally, regarding who is responsible for this certification, how it is done, and the nature of the certification authority or trust.

More important, any effort at certification can address only one aspect of the problem of information on the Internet. After all, the problem is not really so much about unreliable information on the Internet as about people being misled by what is on the Internet. Being misled requires two elements: unreliable information and credulity. Information has no significance unless it is believed. If people easily believe nearly everything they see on the Web, then the element of gullibility must be added to the problem about the quality of the information on the Web. In this regard, it is worth noting that according to one report, about half of Internet users "believe that most or all online information is reliable and accurate."

This suggests that we need to consider people's behavior as consumers of information, or as knowers. If everyone were more careful about what they glean from the Internet, if they were more responsible searchers of information, then perhaps the concerns about unreliable Web sites might be of much less significance. What is it to be a responsible searcher on the Internet?

The Responsibility of Information Seekers

Believing something just because it is on the Web is irresponsible, but maintaining a thorough skepticism regarding everything on the Web is hardly better. One must develop appropriate habits for assessment and use of information on the Internet. A considerable literature has arisen on how to do just that, including some quite practical advice on how to evaluate Web sites. One can even find Web sites devoted to explaining how to evaluate Web sites. Much of the advice is simple common sense: check the source, look for independent confirmation of the information, and so on. The overall lesson is that a responsible information seeker is not passive.

The importance of active involvement in evaluating information becomes especially clear when one examines the behavior of information seekers using the Internet. While many people go to certain trusted Web sites to get information, the most common way people get information on the Internet is by using a search engine. In fact, some sources claim that more than 80 percent of users get their information from search engines.

By typing a few keywords or even a question, a search engine will proceed to identify those Web sites that more or less match the keywords or question. Although the precise workings of many search engines are closely guarded trade secrets, search engines generally operate in one of two ways: they either examine a proprietary database of (selected) Web sites, which they periodically update, or they "crawl" through the World Wide Web, using various algorithms to identify Web sites that meet the search criterion. Using either type of search method, the result commonly yields tens, hundreds, even thousands of identified sites. Such large results are usually of little significance, since they are ranked by order of relevance and few people ever examine search results beyond the first dozen or so listings.

One might argue that the availability of search engines helps people be responsible information seekers on the Internet. For example, anyone can easily determine whether different Web sites report the same information; one can even determine whether certain Web sites have been subject to praise or blame for the information posted on the site. In contrast, few people have the time, resources, or inclination to see how the same story is reported in different newspapers. Unless some reason for doubt arises, usually they believe the reports of their favorite newspapers. But no source of information dominates online, and checking information or its source is fairly effortless using search engines.

Despite these advantages, however, search engines have their own problems. Many search engines are subject to deliberate bias. Some search engines are commercial ventures in which sites must pay for inclusion in their database. Even if inclusion in the database is not for sale or the search engine does not employ a proprietary database, the ranking of results may well be for sale. The popularity of a site depends in large measure on whether it ranks as the first—most "relevant"—site or as the last, least relevant, one. A site that pays for the privilege of a top rank can become a dominant source of information on a particular topic. Imagine a newspaper that determined what appeared on the front page based in part on the financial contribution the source of information paid for the prominence. Just as a practice of selling off the front page would raise questions about a newspaper's trustworthiness, a practice of payment for search result rankings would raise questions about the trustworthiness of results presented in search engines.

Another serious problem with search engines is that they are limited in various ways. These limitations are not simply a matter of how much of the World Wide Web the search engine is searching—though it is important to note that at present no search engine can search the entire Web. Another type of limitation arises from the approximations used to identify Web sites. For example, many search engines identify sites by determining whether the keywords appear on the site. One might reasonably expect that if a Web page contains a particular phrase, then in all likelihood the site is about the topic suggested by that phrase. Plainly, however, although this thinking is reasonable, it carries no guarantee. A search on the phrase "breast cancer" will yield a list of sites that appear to be devoted to information on breast cancer. However, included in the list will be sites containing irrelevant information—for instance, one might be directed to a Web site devoted to an entirely different topic but which states somewhere that the site owners have given to a breast cancer charity. Sophisticated devices designed to fine-tune searches—such as Boolean operators, which can construct more complex search criteria—may reduce, but cannot eliminate, the selection of irrelevant sites.

A different type of limitation of search engines is their determination of appropriate ranking of results in terms of relevancy (ignoring the more evident problem of relevancy rank for sale). Among the criteria that may be used to determine rank are the numbers of times the keywords occur in the site, whether the keywords occur in the site's address or URL, or whether the keywords occur in links from the site or in links to the site. Although each of these criteria may be useful, they are only approximations. It is easy to imagine a less informative site scoring higher in terms of relevancy because of these admittedly superficial criteria.

It is important to keep in mind that a search engine is not a "truth engine." No matter how good the search engine is in selecting the right sites, it cannot attest to the reliability of the information on that site. Wittgenstein in *On Certainty* presents the image of someone trying to check a story in a newspaper by buying other copies of the same newspaper and reading the story again. The absurdity of this effort is plain. It would hardly be less absurd if the individual buys different newspapers, all of which use the same source of information, such as a wire-service report or a press release. But this is more or less what an Internet information seeker could wind up doing. Because information can spread rapidly and globally on the Internet, even the information from a single, unreliable source can appear quickly on many different Web sites, and checking different sites may afford no better test of reliability than buying many copies of the same newspaper, or newspapers that rely on the same wire-service report. In short, using a search engine to check the reliability of information on a Web site has its flaws.

The World Wide Web is still young and, as it evolves and as search engine technology is refined, one can expect many of these limitations to diminish although not entirely disappear. Better search engine technology will likely increase public reliance on the Internet as the prime source of information. However, heavy reliance on search engines—even if searches become more relevant and rankings increase in trustworthiness—raises other difficulties.

The Problem of Reliance

Many observers have noted that Internet use can be customized to suit a variety of needs and desires. Not only can I choose an online newspaper, but I can also modify it in dramatic ways. I can specify that news items within my chosen topics appear on the "front page." News on topics I have little or no interest in can be shifted to the end or even filtered out entirely. As one writer remarks, instead of the *New York Times,* the *Washington Post,* or CNN, I can have "The Daily Me." The significance of this customization, carried to an extreme, is twofold: first, by allowing one person's knowledge of what is news to be so different from another's, the potential for common experiences essential to a sense of community may be drastically reduced, if not undermined entirely. And second, customized news services can foster a polarization, if not an extremism, in opinions, which, in turn, can threaten democratic deliberation. Let me expand upon these two features.

The commentators who have written on the threat to community and democracy posed by the customization of Web experiences—particularly, Cass Sunstein and Andrew Shapiro—generally direct their attention to filters. They argue that if we get our information entirely from the Internet and if we impose perfect filters—so that we exclude from our sight topics we are not interested in—then we run the risk of communities fragmenting along narrow lines of interest. Since it is important to be informed not only of what you want to know but also of what you may not (at first) want to know, news services perfectly filtered by, in effect, consumer preferences can have a devastating effect on the survival of democratic communities.

Communities consist of people with a variety of interests, concerns, and viewpoints, and any effort to reduce that diversity is often seen as repressive and undemocratic. Nevertheless, many writers have argued that democratic communities require the existence of public spaces or forums, accessible by all. Without a public space, the potential for community members to encounter other members with different viewpoints is diminished or eliminated. It is then a short step for one to lose all sense of the many and diverse interests that inform the community's interests.

This loss of community, in turn, can lead to polarization since, if all one hears are echoes of one's own concerns, then one can easily come to believe, from their repetition, that these concerns are the most important—perhaps the only—concerns. When one becomes oblivious to the interests and viewpoints of others, one becomes incapable of deliberation, since when a community deliberates about a course of action, the various interests and viewpoints of its members must be respectfully acknowledged in order for the deliberation to proceed in a fair and democratic manner. If news is customized to exclude all other concerns but one's own, it becomes all the more difficult to recognize these concerns when one must join together in public deliberation.

One response to the problem of fragmentation and polarization is the suggestion that, as more people spend time on the Internet and learn from it what is going on in the world, public spaces must be created on the Internet itself. If the more traditional public spaces—such as parks, public squares, even sidewalks—become less significant, as people occupy more time in cyberspace, then, so the argument goes, we need to create an "e-commons."

Filters and Search Engines

Many of the same problems regarding filters are apparent when one thinks about the increasing reliance on search engines. This becomes clear by realizing that a search engine is the mirror image of a filter. Whereas filters try to exclude what you do not want, search engines try to include only what you do want. At the limit, where filters and search engines are perfect and make no mistake, the theoretical differences between them begin to disappear. Moreover, in some ways, worries about search engines appear more urgent. The main use of filters on the Internet is to eliminate material unsuitable for children; filters for adult use are not common. In contrast, as we mentioned earlier, the use of search engines is widespread.

To be sure, hardly anyone at present relies exclusively on search engines for their information, and for a variety of reasons, including the novelty and imperfections of the technology. But suppose, for the sake of argument, that we are at the limit—search engines can handle extremely sophisticated search criteria, successfully selecting only wanted items. Suppose also that a significant number of people get all of their information from search engines. In that case, it is unlikely that these individuals would search for information on topics in which they have no interest or find uncomfortable. As a consequence, biases regarding the urgency of one's own concerns are thus reinforced, and blindness toward the concerns of others encouraged.

It might be helpful to think about the fragmentation problem in a more general way. Geography fragments the human population, and, to a rough extent, many traditional communities arise from this fragmentation. Since traditional communities are local, many of the virtues found in them arise from the habits that members of a community must develop in order to cooperate with one another to benefit themselves and the community.

The Internet, however, can induce fragmentation along lines that cut across geography, undermining traditional communities. One type of fragmentation encouraged by the Internet is "associational," which results when individuals form associations with others who are very much like them, without regard to geography and perhaps at the expense of associations constrained by geography. Associations of like-minded people—custom communities—do not have to foster habits of tolerance or democracy. Another type of fragmentation encouraged by the Internet is "informational," which, as I have argued, is the consequence of an exclusive reliance on search engines—we become better informed about topics of our choosing, but at the expense of our being informed about topics that matter to others.

Political scientist Robert Putnam suggests that associational fragmentation might be the greater threat to traditional communities. He may be right, but the influences of informational and associational fragmentation are likely to be mutually reinforcing and their bad effects compounded. Further, informational fragmentation can also exacerbate problems within any subgroup that relies on specialized information. Specialization in the sciences, for instance, is efficient for research and training, since an intellectual division of labor allows scientists to focus their energies on narrowly defined problem sets.

But divisions and specializations in the sciences often reflect more the various histories of particular professions and scholars than they do any objective divisions in nature. Consequently, specialization can inhibit progress and creativity because a narrow focus at times is tantamount to tunnel vision. Too often scientists become divorced from the stimulation of interaction with scientists and scholars from neighboring fields. The Internet aids specialization by putting the scientist in touch with like-minded scientists, regardless of geography. But this new interaction comes at the expense of scientists interacting with the broader community of scholars, and the result is ever more fragmented science.

At this point, we should reconsider the earlier supposition that search engines serve as the exclusive source of information for most people. That supposition might seem simply unrealistic since there is no evidence that search engines will come to displace all other sources of information. Furthermore, customization of information sources seems to occur to some extent already in traditional sources. Many traditional sources—for example, newspapers, radio, and television stations—have, or appear to have, biases or ideologies that shape how information is presented; many people choose which source to read, listen to, or watch because they are comfortable with its bias. People with right-wing ideologies usually do not read left-wing magazines, and vice versa. Thus, we seem to have an informational fragmentation even without the Internet. Consequently, the worry that the use of search engines specifically—and the use of the Internet more generally—will lead to informational fragmentation seems overblown: it is based on an unrealistic premise regarding Internet use and it ignores the informational fragmentation that we already encounter prior to the Internet.

One can begin to respond to both points by noting that fragmentation comes in degrees. We do already have some informational fragmentation due, in part, to consumer choices among traditional information sources. And some degree of fragmentation is no doubt beneficial, as is some degree of specialization in the sciences. But informational fragmentation does not have to be complete in order for it to worry us. Nor does the existence of some informational fragmentation mean that we need not be concerned about that fragmentation increasing. We need to be aware of the potential costs of our growing use of search engines, including the loss of less targeted sources of information. If we (choose to) become increasingly less informed about topics that we have no interest in, then significant "stress fractures" in associations and community are a likely result.

This chapter does not pursue the question of how much fragmentation is too much—and perhaps that question allows for little empirical precision. The conclusion one can draw is that we should now cultivate some awareness of the dangers of informational fragmentation rather than take a wait-and-see attitude until some critical threshold has been crossed. We also need to explore suggestions for developing search engines that effectively respond to these concerns. For example, search engines might include information that is not picked up by the intended search but also is not confused with it—such as banner news. A variation on this suggestion would be search engines embedded in general information Web sites: calling up a search engine involves accessing the front page of an online newspaper. Such suggestions are not without problems. What is the incentive for search engine owners to agree to such inclusions? Wouldn't such inclusions simply underscore the worry about bias? Wouldn't some of the questions about certification be applicable here as well?

The question of the reliability of information on the Internet points to both a narrow and a wide issue. The narrow issue concerns whether the information on Internet sites is reliable; the wide issue concerns the impact of a heavy reliance on Internet search engines as sources of information. While more attention must be given to the narrow issue, if we are to realize the benefits of reliable information on the Internet, we must address the wide issue as well.

This chapter was based on an earlier work in *The Report from the Institute for Philosophy & Public Policy*, volume 20, fall 2000.

Sources

Oxford English Dictionary (Oxford, 1971); M. Schroeder, R. Simon, and A. Elstein, "Teenage Trader Runs Afoul of the SEC as Stock Touting Draws Charges of Fraud," *Wall Street Journal* (September 21, 2000); G. Kolata, "Web Research Transforms Visit to the Doctor," *New York Times* (March 6, 2000); "German 'Quack Healer' Sentenced," *Lancet*, vol. 350 (1997); A. Shapiro, *The Control Revolution* (Century Foundaton/Public Affairs, 1999); for further discussion on the idea of seals of approval, see G. Eysenbach and T. Diepgen, "Towards Quality Management of Medical Information on the Internet: Evaluation, Labelling, and Filtering of Information," *British Medical Journal*, vol. 317 (1998); UCLA Internet Report, "Surveying the Digital Future," which is available at www.ccp.ucla.edu/pages/Internet-report.asp; J. Alexander and M. Tate, *Web Wisdom: How to Evaluate and Create Information Quality on the Web* (Erlbaum Associates, 1999); among the sites that offer advice about how to evaluate Web sites, see www.library.george town.edu/internet/eval.htm and www2.widener.edu/Wolfgram-Memorial-Library/webevaluation/examples.htm; for a listing of various statistics on Internet search engine use, see www.searchenginewatch.com/reports/seindex.html; for further information on the sale of search engine result rankings, see www.bigwhat.com/htmldocs/addurl.htm#penny; L. Introna and H. Nissenbaum, "The Politics of Search Engines," *IEEE Computer*, vol. 33 (2000); L. Wittgenstein, *On Certainty* (Blackwell, 1969); N. Negroponte, *Being Digital* (Knopf, 1995); for discussions concerning the point that democratic communities require the existence of public spaces accessible to all, see: A. Chin, "Making the World Wide Web Safe for Democracy: A Medium-Specific First Amendment Analysis," *Hastings Communications & Entertainment Law Journal*, vol. 19 (1997) and also: D. Zatz, "Sidewalks in Cyberspace: Making Space for Public Forums in the Electronic Environment," *Harvard Journal of Law & Technology*, vol. 12 (1998). This issue is also discussed in a forthcoming book by C. Sunstein, *Republic.com* (Princeton University Press, 2001); L. Friedland and Harry Boyte, "The New Information Commons: Community Information Partnerships and Civic Change" (1999), and available at www.publicwork.org/commons/commons.htm; for some efforts in developing the mathematical models of these types of fragmentation, see M. Van Alstyne and E. Brynjolfsson, "Electronic Communities: Global Village or Cyberbalkans?" (1996), and available at www.web.mit.edu/marshall/www/InfoAccess.html; R. Putnam, *Bowling Alone: The Collapse and Revival of American Community* (Simon and Schuster, 2000); M. Van Alstyne and E. Brynjolfsson, "Could the Internet Balkanize Science?" *Science*, vol. 274 (1996).

LEEDS METROPOLITAN
UNIVERSITY
LIBRARY

Do Hackers Provide a Public Service?

Verna V. Gehring

I am sort of a gadfly . . . and the state is like a great and noble steed who is tardy in his motions owing to his very size, and requires to be stirred to life.

—Plato, *Apology*

These days hardly anyone is surprised to receive a high priority e-mail message from the office information technology specialist warning that a computer virus is loose in the network. The risk of computer viruses, which hijack e-mail address books and erase drives, is now a routine part of work life. Most of us respond to office alerts with a sigh; we might turn on a quarantine protocol and perhaps mutter an oath about "hackers" before resuming our workday. Typically, news reports soon detail the extent of the damage caused by the virus, and we might later hear that a suspect has been arrested—somewhere in the world.

Media reports commonly refer to "hackers" as responsible for these exploits. After discussing some recent cases of cybercriminal behavior and legal responses, I will briefly describe the history of hackers and draw distinctions among several kinds of contemporary computer enthusiasts. After arguing that the term "hacker" is used imprecisely and too broadly, I contend that hackers possess ethical scruples that both guide their lives and also serve the public interest.

43

Recent Exploits of Computer Vandals

News stories abound concerning those who illegally gain access to credit card information and go on to charge thousands of dollars, or who commit corporate espionage by computer and cost millions in lost profits. The losses caused by identity theft can be enormous, but the costs incurred by computer criminals who compromise network systems on a large—even global—scale are far more difficult to calculate. Malicious software programs are now routinely hidden in attachments to e-mail messages with subject headings—such as "The Info. You Requested" or "Hi:Check This!"—that encourage recipients to believe that the e-mails come from friends or trusted colleagues, or are worded in ways that pique the recipients' curiosity. Typically, opening the attachment enables a secret program, or "worm" to send itself to everyone in the victim's e-mail address book, spreading the virus— sometimes worldwide—and bringing network traffic to a halt. Following his arrest in December 1999, David Smith pled guilty to charges in connection with his creation of the "Melissa" virus, and he acknowledged that his program caused $80 million in damage, an estimate that reflects the time spent by systems administrators to clear the virus from affected computers.

Perhaps inspired by "Melissa," in early 2000 the "Love Bug" virus—which one computer security expert described as "'Melissa' on steroids"—spread globally via a similar but more comprehensive e-mail piggyback system. Because the virus replaced media files with copies of itself, the damage was far more extensive—according to some estimates, in excess of US $1 billion. The virus seems to have been unleashed from the Philippines, raising questions about whether the program's creator must answer only to Philippine law—which lacks a well-defined area of computer jurisprudence—or whether he can be held legally accountable in other countries. Finally, computer security specialists have remarked at how few, and relatively unsophisticated, programming skills were needed for the virus to immobilize communication worldwide. The notoriety of the "I Love You" virus has encouraged copycats (such as "Joke," and "Anna Kournikova"— which entice recipients to open what they believe is a humorous attachment, or a photo of the famous tennis star), and it is unclear whether creators of one type of virus might be legally responsible for at least some of the damage caused by subsequent copycat programs.

Legal Responses

Legal responses to computer information tampering or theft are still under development. In the US, the FBI's National Infrastructure Protection Center is responsible for tracking denial-of-service problems and defacement of Web sites. Both tampering and theft crimes fall under Title 18 of the United States Code, which covers damage to a computer "used in interstate or foreign commerce." The maximum penalty under the law is ten years in prison and twice the gross monetary loss to victims. Software theft and piracy are considered copyright infringement, a part of Federal law, and carry as little as $2,500 in fines or as much as three years' probation and $40,000 in fines.

To date, the person who has served the most prison time for computer meddling is Kevin Mitnick, who spent nearly five years in Federal prison for admitting to access device, wire, and computer fraud, and for intercepting electronic communications and copying confidential materials. As part of his plea bargain, Mitnick accepted the government's accusation that he caused in excess of five million dollars in damage; yet his fine was slightly above $4,000.

Congress, vexed by the imaginative activity of cybercriminals, is considering enacting new laws or changing existing ones to better protect computer technology. One proposal, for instance, would double prison sentences, allowing ten years' jail time for a first offense and twenty years for subsequent convictions. Another proposal would ease wiretap laws so that officials could more easily examine data traffic and spot illegal activity. The USA Patriot Act, a sweeping resolution passed by Congress shortly after the events of September 11, 2001 and intended to streamline detection and obstruction of terrorist activity, may increase surveillance of cybercriminal activity as well. And late in 2001, the FBI announced formation of a Cybercrime Division to investigate intellectual property, high-tech, and computer crimes. Although its organizational structure is not yet clear, this division may be part of the National Infrastructure Protection Center (an interagency group that tracks cybercrime), and primarily concerns counterterrorism measures.

A Brief History of Hackers, Crackers, Phreaks, and Others

Although media reports of computer vandalism commonly blame "hackers," this use is imprecise. To understand why, one must look to the history of computer enthusiasts and the lexicon they have developed to detail their pursuits.

The first computer programmers did not call themselves "hackers," which derives from the seventeenth-century "hacker," a "lusty laborer" who harvested fields by dogged and rough swings of his hoe. Many of these early programming enthusiasts came from engineering or physics backgrounds, and were amateur radio or model train hobbyists. But from about 1945 onward (and especially during the creation of the first ENIAC computer) some programmers realized that their expertise in computer software and technology had evolved not just into a profession, but into a *passion*. Not until the 1960s did these extraordinarily devoted and talented programmers describe themselves as "hackers," their term of self-identification capturing the tenacious and methodical nature of inquiry considered essential to technological innovation.

One such group became the heart of the MIT Artificial Intelligence Laboratory, and its influence spread to ARPAnet, created by the Department of Defense in 1969 and precursor of the first transcontinental, high-speed computer network. Stanford University's Artificial Intelligence Laboratory (SAIL) and Carnegie-Mellon University (CMU) also became thriving centers of computer science, artificial intelligence, and ultimately gave rise to the Internet, the Unix and Linux systems, and the World Wide Web, among other accomplishments.

These early programmers also recognized a burgeoning hacker culture, typified by a resentment of bureaucratic hurdles—such as restricted access to computer mainframes and telephone systems—that frustrated their efforts to explore fully the technological systems that so intrigued them. Richard Stallman is today best known for such innovative programs as the text-editor program Emacs, and GNU (which, together with Linux, forms an open source operating system rivaling that offered by Microsoft). Stallman offers a colorful description of the nascent "hacker attitude" at the time he joined the MIT Artificial Intelligence laboratory in 1971:

> Bureaucracy should not be allowed to get in the way of doing anything useful. Rules did not matter—results mattered. Rules, in the form of computer security or locks on doors, were held in total, absolute disrespect. We would be proud of how quickly we would sweep away whatever little piece of bureaucracy was getting in the way, how little time it forced you to waste. Anyone who dared to lock a terminal in his office, say because he was a professor and

thought he was more important than other people, would likely find his door left open the next morning. I would just climb over the ceiling or under the floor, move the terminal out, or leave the door open with a note saying what a big inconvenience it is to go under the floor, "so please do not inconvenience people by locking the door any longer." Even now, there is a big wrench at the AI lab entitled, "the seventh-floor master key," to be used in case anyone dares to lock up one of the more fancy terminals.

The fundamental characteristic of hackers can be distilled into one simple criterion: a hacker is one who enjoys the intellectual challenge of creatively overcoming and circumventing limitations of programming systems and who tries to extend their capabilities. Just as important, hackers insist that "hacker" is a term of respect, which can be conferred only by other hackers on those whose creative skills entitle them to membership in a wider community of proficient enthusiasts.

With this brief history in mind, one can easily see why many hackers insist that their term of self-description has been applied too broadly—commonly referring to *anyone* who seeks to extend or circumvent technological limits. The malicious meddler looking to discover sensitive information by "poking around" is not properly called a hacker since, for one thing, sensitive information is often uncovered not by skill but simply by stumbling upon it. "Crackers" are, according to the hackers who disdain them, no more than unskilled stumblers, petty thieves, and vandals who rely on luck. Further, not all *skilled* enthusiasts are hackers, either. One sort of skilled cracker, a "phreak" (or "phone phreak"), breaks into telephone networks or security systems in order to make free calls or commandeer services. Another kind of cracker, sometimes referred to as "warez" or "warez d00dz," tries to obtain copies of copyrighted software, break the protection on the software, and then globally distribute the pirate program. Ideally, a warez d00d tries to release "0-day warez," copies of commercial software copied, cracked, and re-released on the first day the software is available for retail sale.

While crackers are gatecrashers—for them breaking in, perhaps copying, stealing, or commandeering are ends in themselves—hackers are driven by curiosity and a desire for proficiency, even elegance, in their endeavors. They are typically libertarian in their insistence on access—Stallman refused to allow "fancy terminals" in the A.I. lab to remain locked up—but they tend not to be cavalier about the law. Further, as evidenced by the various codes of ethics hackers have formulated for themselves, they have attempted to convey the normative character of their work and the importance of a personal philosophy to develop their intellectual and moral strength and guide their actions.

The Development of Hacker "Manifestos"

The first thorough discussion of an ethical code for hackers appears in Steven Levy's 1984 work, *Hacker: Heroes of the Computer Revolution.* Levy formulates six criteria that summarize hacker behavior and, to some extent, disclose their general attitude. Although this "code" has been reprinted widely, because it reflects attitudes and technical concerns dating from the 1970s, the first two criteria in particular have seen refinement:

- Access to computers—and anything that might teach you something about the way the world works—should be unlimited and total.
- All information should be free.
- Mistrust authority—promote decentralization.
- Hackers should be judged by their hacking, not bogus criteria such as degrees, age, race, or position.
- You can create art and beauty on a computer.
- Computers can change your life for the better.

At about the same time (in 1986) *Phrack,* the "official" hacker newsletter, published "The Manifesto" intended as a statement of the hacker attitude, which "Doctor Crash" summarized in three principles:

- Hackers reject the notion that "businesses" are the only groups entitled to access and use of modern technology.
- Hacking is a weapon in the fight against encroaching computer technology.
- The high cost of equipment is beyond the means of most hackers, and therefore hacking and phreaking are the only recourse to spreading computer literacy.

Though all of the criteria have been interpreted variously, Levy's first two criteria (and all three of Dr. Crash's) have raised contentious discussion about what is meant by "total" and "free" access to computers and information. Particularly in the 1970s and 1980s, and into the 1990s, some argued that free access should be understood literally—computers and software should be cost free and available to anyone—and, consequently, one is justified in lifting restrictions to access and need feel no twinges of guilt about theft.

Few make this argument any longer, and "free" has come to be understood in a more specialized sense. Richard Stallman, for instance, distributes his Emacs program free of charge with a novel agreement requiring its users to share and improve on the software and then pass along the source code "when you distribute any version of Emacs or a related program, and give the recipients the same freedom that you enjoyed." Other programs, such as GNU-Linux, also rely on this notion of "open source" software—that is, a program's software code is made available for anyone to modify or improve upon. Further, one can sell the "free" software—incorporating modifications that make the software easier to use, offering customization, or even simply supplying the software accompanied by directions for its use. (Again, in selling any open source software, the code must be available for the buyer to modify, perhaps to offer for resale.)

In addition to discussion of what constitutes "free access," among other ethical issues debated by hackers are what it is to cause "damage" or "harm" by one's work, the role of intention—whether someone should be morally responsible for harm caused accidentally (as when one inadvertently erases data), and whether a hacker is responsible for the effects of his or her ignorance or lack of skill. Debates also continue over the ethical appropriateness of covering one's tracks, which may require erasures and alterations of data. Privacy is another important ethical issue discussed by hackers; for instance, they disagree about the circumstances that make access to confidential information permissible and they disagree about whether the standards for ethical access to confidential information are today lower because private information about most US citizens is contained in huge databases and is routinely available for purchase.

Samurai

Hackers also debate the possibility that some of their number, while elite in their programming skills, have decided that one should not, need not, or in some circumstances are absolved from, working in service of the good. Some hackers insist that such "dark-side hackers"—although they work with criminal or malicious intent—are not crackers. ("Dark-side hacker" derives from George Lucas' character Darth Vader, who is "seduced by the dark side of the Force.")

Without resolving the issue of whether hackers are ethically justified in working in the service of a "dark side," hackers tend to agree that one can ethically use the *techniques* of the "dark-side hacker" and the "cracker" to achieve *good* ends. A number of self-professed "good" hackers call themselves "samurai" and model themselves after the historical samurai of Japan (and the "net cowboys" of William Gibson's cyberpunk novels). Samurai are hackers who hire themselves out for legal "electronic locksmith work." A samurai might take part in corporate espionage, aid lawyers pursuing privacy-rights and First Amendment cases, or help track down a cracker. Some samurai profess loyalty to their employers, and disdain vandalism, theft, and any extralegal means of obtaining information. (Two other groups, "sneakers" and "tiger teams," are paid professionals who use cracking techniques to test security.) The evolution of informal but enforced norms (combined with, perhaps, respect for the law—or *most* laws) has led samurai to reject acting as a law unto themselves.

Falling into this class also is, one might reasonably suggest, the work of the steganographer. Steganography (which derives from the Greek for hidden writing or drawing) allows one to embed, inject, or substitute hidden material in an existing computer text, graphic, or music file. Unlike cryptography, in which an encoded message is in plain sight and one needs a decoder ring, say, to interpret the message, in steganography anyone—other than the informed recipient—who looks at, reads, or listens to an encoded file will be unaware of its hidden material. Public interest in steganography has burgeoned since September 11, 2001 with renewed questions about the FBI's Internet monitoring program, Carnivore (which, according to public information about the system, is of limited use in finding such encrypted material) and the National Security Agency's efforts (including, possibly, Echelon, which can capture all telecommunications signals). Hackers might justify their work on samurai grounds—in this case, patriotic loyalty motivates the search for hidden information and the imperatives of national security broaden what is considered lawful.

Hacking as a Public Service

Hackers possess qualities that serve the public and help citizens discern the difference between the splashy, headline-grabbing exploits of the cracker, and the usually more quiet and certainly more useful work of the hacker. The remainder of this article articulates several of the qualities hackers display in their work that also serve the public interest.

Curiosity and a Healthy Skepticism. Hackers find fascinating problems, tackle them with skill, determination, and discipline, and they admire those who work to develop those same qualities. One also encounters frequent reminders to employ the "hands-on imperative" and warnings against "reinventing the wheel." That is, hackers enjoin others to apply their curiosity to the truly novel and noteworthy. Anything that inhibits one from recognizing problems or their possible solutions—out of ignorance, vanity, or lack of access to information that would raise a question or reveal a view as merely conventional—is curiosity misapplied, and a life lived less well than its potential. Furthermore, hackers approach large or authoritative structures with mistrust. But their skepticism is not paranoia—hackers are driven to find out for themselves and to verify conventional truths.

In this hackers are solidly in line with the traditional ethical tenets of the Western philosophical tradition. Many have echoed the belief of Plato and Aristotle that the life of inquiry—a life that requires self-discipline, and often the rejection of accepted tradition—leads not just to knowledge, and being a good person, but to becoming a good citizen as well. These philosophers, as their successors, also insisted that one must remain mindful of the crippling effects of ignorance and vanity. In response to the teachers of his time (and ours) who quizzed their students with rhetorical questions, thereby stifling inquiry, the Renaissance thinker, Michel de Montaigne would frequently ask, "What *do* I know?"—reminding himself that knowledge begins with the recognition of one's own ignorance and acceptance of mere convention. Only then can one find the roots of true knowledge.

Autonomy and Responsibility. Related to the ethical injunction to ground our knowledge is the imperative that we must exercise our autonomy and shape our lives according to our own ends. One interpretation of the hacker's command to "hate boredom," for instance, is that hackers accept that self-actualization is one's own responsibility. Any condition of life that one finds unsatisfactory—as Jean-Paul Sartre or a number of existentialists are well known for insisting—one should not endure, and one certainly should not simply hope that someone else will bring relief. The source of dissatisfaction should be eliminated immediately, and by oneself. Boredom and apathy are symptoms of one's ceasing to ask the right questions and proposing alternative solutions; instead, one has abandoned the responsibility for self-reliance.

Although hackers tend to have a libertarian streak, the insistence on autonomy and responsibility does not mean that we may ignore obligations to others and our wider community. Instead, the hacker attitude that directs energy to finding new problems and novel solutions also accepts that dissatisfaction with the status quo and with one's own efforts at effecting change signal the lack of effort, or misapplied efforts, which are one's personal responsibility to correct.

Mutual Aide and Public Involvement. Although debate continues about "free access" in the sense of what ought to be free of cost, the hacker attitude of "free access" also suggests the notion that one ought not hoard what one learns. Just as curiosity often leads to utility, giving—as many classic morality tales conclude—often leads to getting. Hackers tend to share what they know and to help others, learning and being helped in return.

When we share and help, we tend to work in transparency—everyone can see what we are doing, which can have mixed consequences. One good result of transparancy is that, since the term "hacker" is a compliment within the community of hackers, if one has the skills, competence, and—as I argue—the ethics of a hacker—one's peers recognize one for those attributes.

But another consequence of transparency tends not to be celebratory. When hackers work openly, their results are for all to see. When those results embarrass others—revealing their incompetence, laziness, pridefulness, or ignorance, for instance—the natural human response tends to be an attempt to silence the source of the disclosure. In his defense against charges that he was a traitor to Athens, Socrates famously made just that claim, suggesting that by revealing the proud and wrongheaded views of his peers—many of whom also held political power—he guaranteed personal attack. Although Socrates crafted his role as the "gadfly" of Athens, biting and pricking the minds of his fellow citizens, the tendency to respond defensively to embarrassment remains.

The success of both types of technology enthusiasts—both darkside hackers and crackers, as well as the self-professed "good" hackers of various types—at times rely on the ignorance of others. For instance, dark-side hackers (and crackers) exploit human weakness and gullibility to gain access to sensitive information. They might trick others into revealing their bank account passwords (by, for instance, telephoning an intended victim and posing as a field service representative with an urgent access problem). The success of samurais and other "good" hackers also depends as much on human gullibility, ignorance, and laziness as on their own skill. For instance, the samurai who reads the deleted e-mail messages of those employees who work on sensitive areas and unwittingly divulge useful information would see vulnerabilities within the organization better than the employees themselves. In short, weaknesses in "wetware"—in thinking—rather than in software aid the work of both the good and the bad. The "I Love You" virus illustrates perfectly what some call "social engineering"—that is, vulnerabilities in human psychology. The "I Love You" virus relied on human weakness—in this case vanity—for its successful dissemination. Most who receive such a message would not be able to resist opening the file in hopes of learning the identity of their admirer.

Knowledge transforms and can elevate, but not all knowledge is knowledge of the good. Although knowledge can be put to bad use, however, the Western philosophical tradition has also insisted that full knowledge requires full understanding of its application—both its good and bad uses. When Renaissance thinker and master political strategist Niccolo Machiavelli called on a ruler to be both a fox and a lion, he suggested that it was inadequate to have knowledge of only the noble and good. One also had to know the ways of the fox, in order to both complete one's knowledge and eliminate the possibility that one could be fooled by another fox. And to *know* good and bad but *choose* the good gives real moral worth to one's actions.

These elements go a long way in explaining the reputation of hackers. In using the term too broadly, we confuse hackers with crackers. And even in their proper role, since gadflies sometimes act as foxes, we are irritated and at the same time fooled by them.

An Aesthetic Life. A final characteristic, one difficult to describe, concerns the hacker attitude toward life. Some hackers express this attitude as the belief that "computers change life for the better," and that one can "create art and beauty on a computer."

Though hackers believe that computers are a necessary part of the search for the good life—they typically urge proficiency in specific programs (html is a must, according to many accounts), insist that one write open source software and help test and debug the software of others, and encourage the dissemination of useful information—the *spirit* of their advice is to strive to know and to share one's knowledge.

One hacker, who wrote an online primer on hacking (thereby following the dictum that one publish useful information) also suggests
ways to develop one's style and approach to being a hacker. Eric
Raymond (who is the author of, among other works, the *Jargon File*,
an encyclopedic work about hacking and programming) advises
reading widely, studying philosophy (especially the Eastern traditions), developing an appreciation for music, and seeking to refine
one's ear for wordplay and puns. Above all, Raymond enjoins, a hacker must write well in order to clarify his or her thoughts and communicate them effectively. Raymond also follows his additional advice to
not use silly or grandiose user identification names; he simply uses his
own name.

Clearly, this is good advice for anyone. Thinking about these
attributes, one sees a fundamental difference between hackers—who
build—and everyone else, such as crackers, who destroy and trespass
for its own sake, or people like me—novice users of the computer
who use but make no contribution. It's not always easy to see an act
as one of destruction or creation. Did Socrates create or destroy?
Knowledge of the full consequences of one's actions is a tall order.

This chapter was based on an earlier work in *Philosophy & Public
Policy Quarterly,* volume 22, summer 2002.

Sources

For just one example of illegal credit access, see usdoj.gov/criminal/
cybercrime/diekman4.htm; and for information concerning corporate
espionage involving computer access, see "'Netspionage' Costs Firms
Millions," msnbc.com/new, posted September 11, 2001; for information about the David Smith case, see "Smith Pleads Guilty to Melissa
Virus Charges," by Erich Luening, news.cnet.com; for one account of
the "Love Bug" virus and its connection to the Philippines, see
"Computer Virus Hits Businesses, Governments Around the World,"
by K. S. O'Donoghue, www.foxnews.com; on Federal law concerning
software theft, see for instance, 17 U.S.C. §301(a). Among the numerous
sites devoted to Kevin Mitnick, see www.takedown.com; *2600-The
Hacker's Quarterly,* and the "official" Kevin Mitnick site at kevinmit-
nick.com. The USA Patriot Act was introduced as H.R. 3162, and was
passed October 24, 2001. On the source of the word "hacker," see the
Oxford English Dictionary, 1971 edition (volume 1), page 1237. As part
of the history of hackers, some have distinguished among prehacker
"Real Programmers," and first-, second-, and now third-generation
hackers; for discussions on these various subgroups, see "A Brief

History of Hackerdom," which can be found among the writings of Eric Raymond at www.tuxedo.org; also Steve Mizrach, "Is there a Hacker Ethics for 90s Hackers?" copyright 1997 and posted on www.infowar.com; also Steven Levy, *Hackers: Heroes of the Computer Revolution* (Delta, 1984). Richard Stallman describes his life and work at www.stallman.org; his description of the atmosphere at MIT is quoted from project.cyberpunk.ru/-idb/hacker_ethics.html. Some have argued that one can be a hacker in a variety of areas, not just computer and information technology. For an example of this argument, see Pekka Himanen, *The Hacker Ethic and the Spirit of the Information Age* (Random House, 2001). For a useful discussion of hackers, and distinctions among types of computer enthusiasts, see Eric S. Raymond's (esr@snark.thyrus.com) work at, among other places, www.tuxedo.org; also a variety of hacker terminology can be found in the *Jargon File*, created by Eric Raymond and maintained at www.jargon.org. The *Jargon File* relied on in this article is *Jargon File 4.2.0*, dated January 31, 2000; for hacker codes, see Steven Levy's, *Hacker*, Dr. Crash, volume 1, issue 6, phile 3 of 13, "The Techno-Revolution," www.phrack.org. Dr. Crash goes on to insist that every hacker must also be a phone phreak, "because it is necessary to utilize the technology of the phone company to access computers far from where they live. The phone company is another example of technology abused and kept from people with high prices." For excerpts from a number of hacker codes of ethics, see Mizrach article. The copy available was last modified on June 7, 2000. Although numerous versions of hacker ethics abound, most restate Levy, and make additions or revisions. For instance, a 1998 version of the hacker ethics, which identifies itself as the code of the MIT community, adds that, in addition to causing no damage, hacker's work should "be funny, at least to most of the people who experience it." See hacks.mit.edu/Hacks/misc/ethics.html (March 28, 1998 version). On Richard Stallman's novel agreement regarding open source software, see: www.gnu.ai.mit.edu/copyleft. Some might claim that a special case of samurai is the "hactivist" whose aims are ideological. Hacktivists typically justify computer sabotage as necessary to promote political ends. The Pakistan Hackerz Club, for instance, advocates an India-free Kashmir, and has made regular attacks on American and Indian Internet sites (such as Lackland Air Force Base, in Texas), inserting a "Save Kashmir" message. Another common technique is "pinging," that is, one computer repeatedly calls another, shutting down its connections. As one might imagine, as tension between China and Taiwan has grown, programmers on both sides of the Taiwan Strait have plagued the sites of the other, tying up networks and displaying messages in support of one or the other regime. For a useful discussion of recent "hacktivist" activities, see "School for Hackers," Adam Cohen, *Time* (May 22, 2000). Plato's quote concerning Socrates as gadfly of the state is found in the *Apology*: "I am sort of a gadfly . . . and the state is like a great and noble steed who is tardy in his motions owing to his very size, and requires to be stirred to life." Machiavelli's discussion of the importance of knowledge and cunning is found in the *Prince*, chapter 18.

Social Bonds:
Stronger or Weaker?

II

The Impact of the Internet on Civic Life: An Early Assessment

William A. Galston

Suppose that in the summer of 1952 someone had convened a conference on the rise of television and the future of community. The sym-
posiasts would have faced two crucial problems. First, social reality
was moving faster than empirical scholarship. Television was diffusing
at an explosive rate, from being a relative rarity in the late 1940s to near
ubiquity only a decade later. In 1952 scholars studying the social effects
of television might have noted, for example, how neighbors crowded
into a living room to watch the only set on the block, and they might
have drawn conclusions about the medium's community-reinforcing
tendencies that would seem antique only a few years later.

The second difficulty would have been even harder to cope with.
Reasoning by analogy from, for example, the automobile's effects on
sexual morality in the 1920s, these scholars might have suspected that
television's unintended consequences would turn out to be at least as
significant as its directly contemplated purposes. They would have
been hard pressed, however, to move much beyond this general
insight to hypotheses with predictive power. The insertion of a powerful new communications medium into a complex social system was
bound to reconfigure everything from intimate relations to the distribution of public power. But how, exactly?

According to social and political theorist Alan Ehrenhalt, the front
stoop was one of the centers of social life in Chicago's blue-collar

neighborhoods of the early 1950s. During that decade, however, the penetration of television into nearly every home affected not only the dissemination of news and entertainment but also patterns of social interaction. Families spent more time clustered around the television set and less time talking with their neighbors on the street. The increased atomization of social life, in turn, had important ripple effects. Spontaneous neighborhood oversight and discipline of children became harder to maintain, and less densely populated streets opened the door for increased criminal activities.

I do not mean to suggest (nor does Ehrenhalt) that television was solely responsible for these changes; the advent of air-conditioning also helped depopulate streets by making the indoors far more habitable during the dog days of summer. I do want to suggest that the present is for the Internet roughly what 1952 was for television, and that the methodological problems just sketched are the ones we face today.

In the face of such challenges, it is natural, perhaps inevitable, that our thought will prove less flexible and our imagination less capacious than the future we seek to capture. In our mind's eye, we may hold constant what will prove to be most mutable. One of my favorite examples of this (there are many) comes from an article published in the *St. Louis Globe Democrat* in 1888:

> The time is not far distant when we will have wagons driving around with casks and jars of stored electricity, just as we have milk and bread wagons at present. The arrangements will be of such a character that houses can be supplied with enough stored electricity to last twenty-four hours. All that the man with the cask will have to do will be to drive up to the back door, detach the cask left the day before, replace it with a new one, and then go to the next house and do likewise.

As communications expert Carolyn Marvin points out, this vision of the future reflects the assumption of, and hope for, the continuation of the economically and morally self-sufficient household, unbeholden to outside forces, productively and privately going about its own business—a way of life undermined by the very patterns of distribution and concentration that electrical power helped foster.

I draw two lessons from this cautionary example. First, in speculating about the impact of the Internet on community life, we should be sensitive to the often surprising ways in which market forces can shape emerging technologies to upset entrenched social patterns. (This maxim is particularly important for an era such as ours in which the market is practically and ideologically ascendant.) Second, we should be as conscious as possible of the cultural assumptions and trends that shape the way we use, and respond to, new technologies such as the Internet. In this connection, I want to suggest that contemporary American society is structured by two principal cultural forces: the high value attached to individual choice and the longing for community.

Choice and Community

Scholars in a range of disciplines have traced the rise during the past generation of choice as a core value. Market research expert Daniel Yankelovich suggests that what he calls the "affluence effect"—the psychology of prosperity that emerged as memories of the Depression faded—weakened traditional restraints: "People came to feel that questions of how to live and with whom to live were a matter of individual choice not to be governed by restrictive norms. As a nation, we came to experience the bonds to marriage, family, children, job, community, and country as constraints that were no longer necessary."

In Alan Ehrenhalt's analysis, the new centrality of choice is a key explanation for the transformation of Chicago's neighborhoods since the 1950s. Stanford School of Law Professor Lawrence Friedman argues that individual choice is the central norm around which the modern American legal system has been restructured. Social and political theorist Alan Wolfe sees individual choice at the heart of the nonjudgmental tolerance that characterizes middle-class morality in contemporary America.

The problem (emphasized by all these authors) is that as individual choice expands, the bonds linking us to others tend to weaken. To the extent that the desire for human connections is a permanent feature of the human condition, the expansion of choice was bound to trigger an acute sense of loss, now expressed as a longing for community. (The remarkable public response to political theorist Robert Putnam's *Bowling Alone* can in part be attributed to this sentiment.) Few Americans are willing to surrender the expansive individual liberty they now enjoy, however, even in the name of stronger marriages, more stable neighborhoods, or fuller citizenship. This tension constitutes what many Americans experience as the central dilemma of our age: as Wolfe puts it, "how to be an autonomous person and tied together with others at the same time."

I do not believe that this problem can ever be fully solved; to some extent, strong ties are bound to require compromises of autonomy, and vice versa. (This exemplifies Isaiah Berlin's pluralist account of our moral condition: the genuine goods of life are diverse and in tension with one another, so that no single good can be given pride of place without sacrificing others.) Still, there is an obvious motivation for reducing this tension as far as possible—that is, for finding ways of living that combine individual autonomy and strong social bonds.

This desire gives rise to a concept that I call voluntary community. This conception of social ties compatible with autonomy has three defining conditions: low barriers to entry, low barriers to exit, and interpersonal relations shaped by mutual adjustment rather than hierarchical authority or coercion. Part of the excitement surrounding the Internet is what some see as the possibility it offers of facilitating the formation of voluntary communities so understood. Others doubt that the kinds of social ties likely to develop on the Internet can be adequate substitutes, practically or emotionally, for the traditional ties they purport to replace.

Are Online Groups "Communities"?

Writing thirty years ago, information technology pioneers J. C. R. Licklider and Robert Taylor suggested that "life will be happier for the online individual because the people with whom one interacts most strongly will be selected more by commonality of interests and goals than by accidents of proximity." Whether Internet users are in fact happier—and, if so, whether they are happier because they are users—remains to be seen and may never be known (the problems of research design for that issue boggle the mind). The underlying hypothesis that "accidents of proximity" are on balance a source of unhappiness seems incomplete at best. Licklider and Taylor were certainly right, however, to predict that online communication would facilitate the growth of groups with shared interests. Indeed, participation in such groups is now the second most frequently interactive activity (behind e-mail) among online users.

Anecdotal evidence suggests that these groups fill a range of significant needs for their participants. For some, the exchange of information and opinions about shared enthusiasms—rock groups or sports teams, for example—is satisfying as an end in itself. For others, this exchange serves important personal or professional goals. Those suffering from specific diseases can share information about promising doctors, therapies, and treatment centers more widely and rapidly than ever before. A friend of mine who works as the lone archivist in a city library system says that participating in the online group of archivists from around the country mitigates the otherwise intense sense of personal and professional isolation. In this sense, computer-mediated communication can be understood as raising to a higher power the kinds of non-place-based relationships and associations that have existed for centuries in industrialized societies.

But are these shared activities "communities"? What is at stake in this question? One commentator skeptical of the claims of techno-communitarian enthusiasm argues that:

> a community is more than a bunch of people distributed in all 24 time zones, sitting in their dens and pounding away on keyboards about the latest news in alt.Music.indigogirls. That's not a community; it's a fan club. Newsgroups, mailing lists, chat rooms—call them what you will, the Internet's virtual communities are not communities in almost any sense of the word. A community is people who have greater things in common than a fascination with a narrowly defined topic.

Note that this objection revolves around the substance of what members of groups have in common, not the nature of the communication among them. By this standard, stamp clubs meeting face-to-face would not qualify as communities. Conversely, Jews in the Diaspora would constitute a community, even if the majority never meet one another face-to-face, because what they have in common is a sacred text and its competing interpretations as authoritative guides to the totality of temporal and spiritual existence.

To assess these claims, we may begin with Thomas Bender's classic definition of community: "A community involves a limited number of people in a somewhat restricted social space or network held together by shared understandings and a sense of obligation. Relationships are close, often intimate, and usually face-to-face. Individuals are bound together by affective or emotional ties rather than by a perception of individual self-interest. There is a 'weness' in a community; one is a member." Upper-middle-class American professionals tend to dismiss this picture of community as the idealization of a past that never was. Bender insists, however, that it offers a tolerably accurate picture of town life in America before the twentieth century:

The town was the most important container for the social lives of
men and women, and community was found within it. The geo-
graphic place seems to have provided a supportive human surround
that can be visualized in the image of concentric circles. The inner-
most ring encompassed kin, while the second represented friends
who were treated as kin. Here was the core experience of community. Beyond these rings were two others: those with whom one dealt
regularly and thus knew and, finally, those people who were recognized as members of the town but who were not necessarily known.

Personal experience has convinced me that community, so understood, is not merely a part of a vanished past. On a trip to Portugal,
my family stopped for the night at the small town of Condeixa, about
ten miles south of the medieval university town of Coimbra. After
dinner I went to the village square, where I spent one of the most
remarkable evenings of my life. Children frolicked on playground
equipment set up in the square. Parents occupied some of the bench-
es positioned under symmetrical rows of trees; on others, old men sat
and talked animatedly. At one point a group of middle-aged men,
some carrying portfolios of papers, converged on the square and discussed what seemed to be some business or local matter. The square
was ringed by modest cafes and restaurants, some catering to
teenagers and young adults, others to parents and families. From time
to time a squabble would break out among the children playing in the
square; a parent would leave a cafe table, smooth over the conflict,
and return to the adult conversation. As I was walking around the
perimeter of the square, I heard some singing. Following the sound, I
peered into the small Catholic Church on the corner and discovered a
young people's choir rehearsing for what a poster on the next block
informed me was a forthcoming town festival in honor of St. Peter.

Many aspects of this experience struck me forcibly, particularly
the sense of order, tranquility, and human connection based on years
of mutual familiarity, stable social patterns, and shared experience. I
was not surprised to learn subsequently that about half of all young
people born in Portuguese small towns choose to remain there
throughout their adult lives, a far higher percentage than for small-
town youth in any other nation of western Europe.

Bender's examples of community (and my own) are place based,
but it is important not to build place, or face-to-face relationships, into
the definition of community. To do this would be to resolve by fiat, in
the negative, the relationship between community and the Internet.
Instead, I suggest that we focus on the four key structural features of

community implied by Bender's account—namely, limited membership, shared norms, affective ties, and a sense of mutual obligation—and investigate, as empirical questions, their relation to computer-mediated communication.

Limited Membership. Although technical restrictions do exist and are sometimes employed, a typical feature of online groups is weak control over the admission of new participants. Anecdotal evidence suggests that many founding members of online groups experience the rapid influx of newer members as a loss of intimacy and dilution of the qualities that initially made their corner of cyberspace attractive. Some break away and start new groups in an effort to recapture the original experience.

Weak control over membership is not confined to electronic groups, of course. Up to the early 1840s, for example, Boston was conspicuous among American cities for the relative stability and homogeneity of its population, which contributed to what outside observers saw as the communitarian intimacy and solidarity of Boston society. Then, in the single year of 1847, more than 37,000 immigrants arrived in Boston, a city of fewer than 115,000 inhabitants. By the mid-1850s, more than one-third of its population was Irish. Boston was riven, with consequences that would persist for more than a century.

Many kinds of groups can undergo rapid changes of membership, but they may respond differently. In a famous discussion, Albert Hirschman distinguishes between two kinds of responses to discontent within organizations. "Exit" is the act of shifting membership to new organizations that better meet our needs; "voice" is the ability to alter the character of the organizations to which we already belong. Exit is, broadly speaking, marketlike behavior, whereas voice is more nearly political.

I suggest a hypothesis: When barriers to leaving old groups and joining new ones are relatively low, exit will tend to be the preferred option; as these costs rise, the exercise of voice becomes more likely. Because it is a structural feature of most online groups that border crossings are cheap, exit will be the predominant response to dissatisfaction. If so, it is unlikely that online groups will serve as significant training grounds for the exercise of voice—a traditional function of Tocquevillian associations. In Boston, by contrast, because the perceived cost of exit was high, the Brahmins stayed put and struggled with the Irish for a hundred years, a tension that helped develop one of this country's richest political traditions.

In a diverse democratic society, politics requires the ability to deliberate, and to compromise, with individuals unlike oneself. When we find ourselves living cheek by jowl with neighbors with whom we differ but from whose propinquity we cannot easily escape, we have powerful incentives to develop modes of accommodation. On the other hand, the ready availability of exit tends to produce internally homogeneous groups that may not even talk with one another and that lack incentives to develop shared understandings across their differences. One of the great problems of contemporary American society and politics is the proliferation of narrow groups and the weakening of structures that create incentives for accommodation. It is hard to see how the multiplication of online groups will improve this situation.

Shared Norms. A different picture emerges when we turn our attention from intergroup communication to the internal life of online groups. Some case studies suggest that online groups can develop complex systems of internalized norms. These norms arise in response to three kinds of imperatives: promoting shared purposes, safeguarding the quality of group discussion, and managing scarce resources in what can be conceptualized as a virtual commons.

As political theorist Elinor Ostrom has argued, the problem of regulating a commons for collective advantage can be solved through a wide range of institutional arrangements other than private property rights or coercive central authority. Internet groups rely to an unusual degree on norms that evolve through iteration over time and are enforced through moral suasion and group disapproval of conspicuous violators. This suggests that despite the anarcho-libertarianism frequently attributed to Internet users, the medium is capable of promoting a kind of socialization and moral learning through mutual adjustment.

I know of no systematic research exploring these moral effects of group online activities and their consequences (if any) for offline social and political behavior. One obvious hypothesis is that to the extent that young online users come to regard the internal structure of their groups as models for offline social and political groups, they will be drawn to (or demand) more participatory organizations whose norms are enforced consensually and informally. If so, it would be important to determine the extent to which this structure reflects the special imperatives of organizations in which barriers to entrance and exit are low. The ideal of voluntary community reinforced by the

Internet is likely to run up against the coercive requisites of majoritarian politics.

Affective Ties. Proponents of computer-mediated communication as the source of new communities focus on the development of affective ties among online group members. One of the gurus of virtual community, Howard Rheingold, asks whether telecommunication culture is "capable of becoming more than 'pseudocommunity,' where people lack the genuine personal commitments to one another that form the bedrock of genuine community." He defines virtual communities as "social aggregations that emerge from the Net when enough people carry on public discussions long enough, with sufficient human feeling, to form webs of personal relationships."

In this connection, the crucial empirical question is the relation between face-to-face communication (or its absence) and the development of affective ties. How important are visual and tonal cues? How important is it to have some way of comparing words and deeds? Here is one hypothesis: it is impossible to create ties of depth and significance between two individuals without each being able to assess the purposes and dispositions that underlie the other's verbal communications. Is the interlocutor sincere or duplicitous? Does he really care about me, or is he merely manipulating my desire for connection to achieve (unstated) purposes of his own? Does the overall persona an interlocutor presents to me seem genuine or constructed? We all rely on a range of nonverbal evidence to reduce (if never quite eliminate) our qualms about others' motivations and identities.

Internet enthusiasts respond to these questions by deconstructing the ideal of face-to-face communication. They point out (correctly) that duplicity and manipulation have been enduring facts of human history and the advent of computer-mediated communication raises at most questions of degree rather than kind. I must confess that I come away unconvinced. Considerable evidence suggests that the Internet facilitates the invention of online personalities at odds with offline realities and that the ability to simulate identities is one of its most attractive features for many users (gender bending is said to be especially popular). However, the playful exercise of the imagination, whatever its intrinsic merits and charms, is not readily compatible with the development of meaningful affective ties. (Devotees of what might be called postmodern psychology, with its emphasis on social construction and bricolage and rejection of the distinction between surface and depth, might want to quarrel with this. So be it. I see no way of discussing affective ties without invoking some distinction between genuine and spurious emotions and identities.)

Another hotly debated issue is the relation between computer-mediated communication and the tendency to express strong sentiments in antisocial ways. Some researchers have argued that because the absence of visual and tonal cues makes it more difficult to see the pain words can inflict, the Internet reduces restraints on verbal behavior and invites individuals to communicate in impulsive ways. (An analogy would be the asserted desensitizing effects of high-altitude bombing.) Other researchers argue that it is precisely the absence of traditional cues that promotes the formation of social norms for Internet speech and that there is no evidence that this speech is more antisocial on average than is face-to-face communication. Given the fragmentary evidence, I see no way of resolving this debate right now. Speaking anecdotally, the controversy and bitterness stirred up by comments on my synagogue's listserv suggest to me that the pessimists may have the stronger case. Once an initial provocation occurs, the nature of the medium makes it easy to escalate the dispute in ways that might be muted in a face-to-face group. (In the interest of full disclosure, I should note that some members of my synagogue, on the basis of past controversies, believe that face-to-face exchanges on the disputed topics would have been equally uncivil.)

Mutual Obligation. The final dimension of community to be considered is the development of a sense of mutual obligation among members. Recall John Winthrop's famous depiction of the communal ideal aboard the *Arbella*: "We must entertain each other in brotherly affection, we must be willing to abridge ourselves of our superfluities, for the supply of others' necessities. We must delight in each other, make others' conditions our own, rejoice together, mourn together, labor and suffer together." Winthrop's demands may be too stringent, but at the very least community requires some heightened identification with other members that engenders a willingness to sacrifice on their behalf.

The technology critic Neil Postman argues that whatever may be the case with norms and emotions, there is no evidence that participants in online groups develop a meaningful sense of reciprocal responsibility or mutual obligation. Groups formed out of common interests need not develop obligations because by definition the interest of each individual is served by participating in the group. (When that ceases to be the case, it is almost costless to leave the group.) The problem is that bonds created by interests (in either sense of the term) provide no basis for the surrender of interests—that is, for sacrifice.

I find it intriguing that many defenders of online groups concede Postman's factual premise but deny its normative relevance. Communications expert Nessim Watson, for example, argues that communities characterized by a strong sense of mutual obligation have virtually disappeared in contemporary America; to single out online groups for criticism on this score is both unfair and an exercise in nostalgia. Efforts to resuscitate the obsolescent idea of mutual obligation are likely to prove counterproductive: "Those who champion Postman's noble metaphor of community as common obligation are most often faced with the task of dragging other community members kicking and screaming into their part of the obligation. Attempts to construct community usually result in the increased frustration of organizers and the increased cynicism of participants toward the entire idea of community." In late-twentieth-century America, Watson concludes, there is no alternative to voluntary community based on perceptions of individual interest; we will have to get along as best we can without antique norms and practices of sacrifice and mutual obligation.

I very much doubt that our society, or any society, can indefinitely do without these civic virtues. The question of whether emerging forms of group activity help foster these virtues or reinforce their absence is likely to prove significant for the future. The magnitude of the impact will depend in part on the consequences of online activities for more traditional forms of group activity. I now turn to that question.

Online Groups and Place-Based Communities

In the 1996 Survey of Civic Involvement, the American Association of Retired Persons (AARP) explored current community understandings and practices (table 4-1). One of the survey questions asks respondents about their conceptions of community: "We often hear people talking about some community, or about things going on in their communities. If I were to ask you about 'your community' what community would come to mind?" The organization's report on the survey notes that "up to three separate responses were permitted and recorded." Only 15 percent of respondents failed to offer any example of what they considered to be a community.

It is clear from the survey results that for most people, community is still a territorial concept: 35 percent cited village, town, city, or county; 30 percent mentioned neighborhood, subdivision, or street. Overall, 59 percent of the entire sample offered one or more territorial examples of community. Formal organizations and voluntary associations (Tocquevillian America or, if you like, Putnamville) were cited by 34 percent of all respondents. Twenty-nine percent mentioned churches or faith-based organizations; no other type of association was mentioned by as many as 4 percent of respondents. Informal and "abstract" groupings and collectivities also came up frequently, with at least one example cited by 39 percent of all respondents. The authors of the survey note that although numerous respondents mentioned non-place-based examples of community, electronic information groups were conspicuous by their absence:

> Although the majority of respondents say they have used a computer in the past year, computer groups or people with whom they connect by computer were almost never mentioned directly by the respondents. Surely many of them are starting to use their computers and the Internet to communicate with others in their communities, whether geographically or socially defined; but they have not come to think of the computer network itself as a significant form of community in its own right.

Young adults are significantly less likely to cite place-based and formal organizations than are other adults and significantly more likely to cite informal organizations. They are also somewhat more likely to feel distant from all forms of community.

Among the computer users in the sample, those who participated in computer-mediated communication (e-mail or chat groups) ranked significantly lower in community attachment than those who have not done so. This would appear to suggest that for some users, computer-mediated communication serves as a replacement for more traditional, local forms of attachment. On closer inspection, it becomes clear that this result is entirely a function of the fact that young adults are more frequent online users and less attached to localities. The question for the future is whether this pattern will persist as today's cohort of young adults, who have postponed marriage and permanent employment far longer than did their parents and grandparents, enters into the kinds of personal and economic relationships that historically have been correlated with place-based ties.

Table 4-1. Type of Community Cited, by Age Group
Percent

Type of community	18-30	31-49	50-70	71 and older
Place	47.6	63.6	65.0	56.1
Formal organizations	24.5	35.9	39.2	41.1
Informal organizations	54.3	36.2	34.3	23.9
None	18.4	14.3	12.8	17.1

(N= 1,500)

Source: Data from Thomas M. Guterbock and John C. Fries, "Maintaining America's Social Fabric: The AARP Survey of Civic Involvement," University of Virginia, Center for Survey Research, 1997, p. 3.

The AARP survey defines an index of social involvement based on the level of self-reported activity in ten key activities. The average American scored 6.3, the index range being 0 to 19. Sixty-three percent of respondents had used a computer during the past year; they had an average score of 6.7 compared with 5.6 for nonusers. (There was no significant difference between those who used computers for some mode of computer-mediated communication and those who used them for noncommunicative activities such as word processing or solitary games.) After taking age, education, and income into account, the study finds that computer usage had a "[statistically] significant but small effect" on social involvement.

In sum, the AARP survey suggests that online groups have not had a strong generalized effect on either the theory or practice of community in America. There is evidence, however, of shifts among young adults. If this proves to be a generational effect and not merely a life-cycle effect (the jury is still out), then some of the characteristics of online groups discussed earlier in this chapter could over time have a significant impact on American society.

Combining Place and Cyberspace

The discussion thus far has drawn a sharp distinction between place-based and virtual communities. It is possible to combine them (or at least to try) by constructing place-based local networks. The Association for Community Networking estimates that there are now approximately 150 electronic or civic networks. The pioneers of community networking hoped that it would lead to denser connections among local participants and increased civic engagement. These hopes have been fulfilled only in part. In a recent survey, Lee Sproull and John Patterson report that many of the participants in projects designed to encourage community networking:

> Spend most of their time in placeless or remote activity, rather than in activity tied to the local community.... Even in the BEV [Blacksburgh, Virginia, Electronic Village] project, which supports a large number of local business and community Web sites and local discussion groups, respondents report that the project is more help-ful for placeless or remote activity (friends outside Blacksburgh, 84 percent; national interest groups, 54 percent) than for local activity (neighbors, 24 percent; local interest groups, 30 percent).

In short, it has proved surprisingly difficult to enlist modern information technology in the service of place-based communities. Although some intensification of connections among local residents does occur, the dominant effect seems to be the turn away from place toward placeless groups. As we have seen, there are good reasons to believe that the weakening of place-based ties entails substantial social costs and risks. Placeless communities are more likely to be thin communities.

On the other hand, we should be careful not to leap to apocalyp-tic conclusions about the social effects of the Internet, for good or ill. A standard thesis among students of social capital is that group mem-bership tends to increase trust, which in turn enhances the coopera-tive capacities of the larger society. In a careful multivariate analysis of recent survey data, University of Maryland Government and Politics Professor Eric Uslaner casts doubt on these hopes. He finds that involvement in online communities neither builds nor destroys trust. We bring our prior selves, the sum of our socialization, to the Internet; we use it, but it does not transform us. More broadly, there is no smooth path leading from involvement in particular communities (whether based on common place or common interests) and the "gen-eralized social trust"—the ability to cooperate with strangers and those unlike oneself that large modern societies require. Uslaner insists that we are not likely to become more trusting in people unlike ourselves by interacting, online or offline, with people like ourselves. Instead, he concludes, such trust "reflects an optimistic worldview and a belief that others share your fundamental values." The belief that others share our values is linked, in turn, to the sense that they are like us in the most important respects. If so, the increased ethnic heterogeneity of the US population stemming from historically high levels of immigration and the increased economic heterogeneity resulting from emerging patterns of income and wealth distribution may turn out to be more significant determinants of social attitudes than are changes in information technology.

Voluntary Community, Information, and Attitude Formation

I return now to what appears to me to be the central issue in evaluating the likely effect of the Internet on civic life. Many Americans today are looking for ways to reconcile powerful but often conflicting desires for autonomy and connection. The idea of voluntary community draws its appeal from that quest: if we are linked to others by choice rather than accident, if our interaction with them is shaped by mutual adjustment rather than hierarchical authority, and if we can set aside these bonds whenever they clash with our individual interests, then the lamb of connection can lie down with the lion of autonomy. Online groups are paradigmatic examples of voluntary community—whence the enthusiasm they have aroused in many quarters.

It is far too early to know what kinds of effects they will have over time on the relations between individuals and communities in America. However, four kinds of structural doubts can be raised about the civic consequences of voluntary communities: because they give pride of place to exit, they do not promote the development of voice; because they emphasize mutual adjustment, they do not acknowledge the need for authority; because they are brought together and held together by converging individual interests, they neither foster mutual obligation nor lay the basis for sacrifice; and because they bring together people who are alike rather than different in crucial respects, they may intensify current tendencies toward fragmentation and polarization in US civic life. This final point may seem less than obvious than the others; let me expand on it.

To begin, voluntary communities tend to be homogeneous. When given a choice, most people tend to associate with others who are like themselves in the respects they regard as important. Above a relatively low threshold, most people experience deep difference as dissonant and unpleasant. Even when such differences need not be reconciled through explicit collective decisions, they suffuse the shared social space and reduce its appeal for many denizens. To be sure, many people experience differences of food, culture, and even opinion as stimulating, so long as they can sample them at will and leave when they choose. For most people, in short, diversity is a nice place to visit, but they do not really want to live there.

Because Internet communities are voluntary, they are more likely to be homogeneous than heterogeneous, and group homogeneity can have negative consequences. In an important theoretical paper, information technology experts Marshall Van Alstyne and Erik Brynjolfsson show how the Internet can translate even weak preferences for those like one-self into the formation of homogeneous subgroups whose internal inter-actions far exceed cross-group communications, a condition they term "cyberbalkanization." Left unchecked, cyberbalkanization can yield results that are economically efficient (in the sense that no individual can be made subjectively better off by switching from more focused to less focused associations) but socially suboptimal. For example, the growth of hyperspecialized communities can slow the growth of scientific knowledge, which depends on exchanges of data and critical perspec-tives across group boundaries.

In a related analysis, political theorist and communications expert Bruce Bimber suggests that the Internet's probable effect will be the intensification of group-centered politics, a process he terms "acceler-ated pluralism." His argument rests on two empirical premises: first, that the Internet will not alter the fact that most people are highly selective in their attention to issues and information; and second, that the Internet lowers the costs of locating, organizing, and mobilizing communities of like-minded individuals. On the one hand, this devel-opment may be described as democratization of group politics, as reduced transaction costs increase the organizational opportunities of resource-poor individuals and groups. On the other hand, accelerated pluralism decreases political coherence and stability while intensify-ing fragmentation, as narrowly focused "issue publics" form for tran-sitory purposes, exert single-interest pressure on the political system, and dissolve when their task is done. In the process, the power of more traditional public and voluntary sector institutions that enjoy some stability over time and work to integrate (or at least broker) diverse preferences is likely to erode.

The rise of homogeneous communities tends not only to decrease intergroup community and increase political fragmentation but also to exacerbate the difficulty of reconciling diverse interests and world-views. In a recently published book, Cass Sunstein summarizes a wide range of empirical studies, conducted in more than a dozen nations, that point toward a common conclusion: a group of like-minded people who engage in discussion among themselves are likely to adopt the more extreme rather than more moderate variants of the group's shared beliefs. It turns out that particularly high levels of polarization occur when group members meet anonymously, which is precisely what the Internet permits. By contrast, face-to-face discussion within heterogeneous groups is more likely to yield a moderation of views all around or at least an enhanced willingness to listen to evidence and arguments and to alter one's judgments.

Conclusion

In today's cultural climate, the response to these doubts about the civic effects of voluntary communities is easy to anticipate: anything that restricts choice runs the risk of trapping individuals in webs of oppressive relations. What could be worse than that? My answer is this: Learning to make the best of circumstances one has not chosen is part of what it means to be a good citizen and a mature human being. We should not organize our lives around the fantasy that entrance and exit can always be cost free or that we can wall ourselves off from those who are different without paying a long-term social price. Online groups can fulfill important emotional and utilitarian needs, but they must not be taken as solutions for our current civic ills, let alone as comprehensive models of a better future.

This chapter was published in *Governance.com: Democracy in the Information Age,* edited by Elaine Ciulla Kamarck and Joseph S. Nye, Jr. (The Brookings Institution, 2002) and appears here with permission.

Sources

Alan Ehrenhalt, *The Lost City: Discovering the Forgotten Virtues of Community in the Chicago of the 1950s* (Basic Books, 1995); the *St. Louis Globe Democrat* quote can be found in Carolyn Marvin, *When Old Technologies Were New: Thinking about Communications in the Late Nineteenth Century* (Oxford University Press, 1988); Daniel Yankelovich, "How Changes in the Economy Are Reshaping American Values," in *Values and Public Policy,* edited by Henry J. Aaron, Thomas E. Mann, and Timothy Taylor (Brookings, 1994). Lawrence Friedman, *The Republic of Choice: Law, Authority, and Culture* (Harvard University Press, 1990), and Alan Wolfe, *One*

Nation, After All (Viking, 1998)—an influential formulation of this tension is found in Ralf Dahrendorf's *Life Chances: Approaches to Social and Political Theory* (London: Weidenfeld and Nicolson, 1979). A recent survey asked Americans in which decade in the past half century they would most like to have lived, given the choice. In every age cohort, the 1950s proved to be the most popular choice. J. E. C. Licklider and Robert Taylor, quoted in *Virtual Culture: Identity and Communication in Cybersociety,* edited by Steven G. Jones (Thousand Oaks, CA: Sage Publications, 1977); on the growth of online groups, see "Technology and On-line Use Survey" (Pew Research Center for the People and the Press, 1996), cited in Pippa Norris, "Who Surfs? New Technology, Old Voters, and Virtual Democracy in America," and appears in *Democracy.com? Governance in a Networked World,* edited by Elaine Ciulla Kamarck and Joseph S. Nye Jr. (Hollis Publishing, 1999). J. Snyder, "Get Real," *Internet World,* vol. 7, no. 2 (1996); Thomas Bender, *Community and Social Change in America* (Johns Hopkins University Press, 1982); see Doris Kearns Goodwin, *The Fitzgeralds and the Kennedys: An American Saga* (St. Martin's Press, 1987), chap. 3; Margaret McLaughlin, Kerry K. Osborne, and Christine B. Smith, "Standards of Conduct on Usenet," and Nancy K. Baym, "The Emergence of Community in Computer-Mediated Community," both in Steven G. Jones, ed., *Cybersociety: Computer-Mediated Communication and Community* (Thousand Oaks, CA: Sage Publications, 1995); Nessim Watson, "Why We Argue about Virtual Community: A Case Study of the Phish.Net Fan Community" in the *Virtual Culture* volume; Elinor Ostrom, *Governing the Commons: The Evolution of Institutions for Collective Action* (Cambridge University Press, 1990); for a summary and discussion concerning the relation of computer-mediated communication and antisocial expression, see Guiseppe Mantovani, *New Communication Environments: From Everyday to Virtual* (London: Taylor and Francis, 1996); John Winthrop, "A Modell of Christian Charity" (1630), in *The Puritans,* edited by Perry Miller and Thomas H. Johnson (New York: American Book Company, 1938); Neil Postman, *Technopoly: The Surrender of Culture to Technology* (Vintage, 1993); for a discussion of civic virtues, see William A. Galston, *Liberal Purposes: Goods, Virtues, and Diversity in the Liberal State* (Cambridge University Press, 1991), chap. 10; Thomas M. Guterbock and John C. Fries, "Maintaining America's Social Fabric: The AARP Survey of Civic Involvement," University of Virginia, Center for Survey Research, 1997. The AARP survey also finds that computer usage is positively correlated with organizational membership and that among computer users, those who participate in computer-mediated communication on average join more offline groups than those who do not. In addition, computer users are more likely to engage in informal volunteer activities than are nonusers.

These results remain statistically significant after correcting for background variables such as income and education. Lee Sproull and John Patterson, "Computer Support for Local Communities," Stern School of Business, New York University, 2000; Eric Uslaner, "Trust, Civic Engagement, and the Internet," paper presented at the Joint Sessions of the European Consortium for Political Research, Workshop on Electronic Democracy, University of Grenoble, April 6–11, 2000; Marshall Van Alstyne and Erik Brynjolfsson, "Electronic Communities: Global Village or Cyberbalkans?" Sloan School, MIT, March 1997; Bruce Bimber, "The Internet and Political Transformation: Populism, Community, and Accelerated Pluralism," *Polity*, vol. 31 (Fall 1998); Cass Sunstein, *Republic.com* (Princeton University Press, 2001), chap. 3; for related reflections on the theme of the moderation of views in face-to-face discussions, see Peter Levine, "The Internet and Civil Society," *Report from the Institute for Philosophy and Public Policy*, vol. 20 (Fall 2000), pp. 1–8.

The Internet and Civil Society

Peter Levine

Civil society is moving to the Internet. All kinds of organizations use Web pages for recruitment, public relations, fund-raising, and communication among their members. Citizens get their news from Web pages and deliberate about public affairs via e-mail. Parishioners send electronic condolences to bereaved members of their congregations. Hobbyists exchange advice and treasured objects on specialized Internet sites.

But as civil society moves online, some worrying trends are beginning to emerge. This article examines five main grounds for concern: inequality, weakened social bonds, diminished public deliberation, rampant consumerism, and the impact of eroding privacy on freedom of association. The purpose of this paper is not to issue dire predictions. The Internet may prove beneficial to civil life—but that does not justify ignoring potential risks.

Equity

The first (and most widely recognized) reason to worry about the effect of the existing Internet on civic life is that people cannot use computers effectively unless they have money and skills and access to high-speed connections. In the United States, income, race, education, and age (but not gender) predict whether people use computers and computer networks.

During the Clinton Administration, this "Digital Divide" was a major focus in Washington. With bipartisan support, Congress passed the E-Rate tax, which subsidizes wiring schools; the Technology Opportunities Program (TOP), which promotes the use of digital technologies in government and the nonprofit sector; and the Community Technology Centers Program, which underwrites programs in poor urban and rural areas. Things changed rapidly with the election of President Bush; the new administration proposed ending the various federal programs that were aimed at bridging the Digital Divide.

The reason for this shift was ideology, but bolstered by eye-catching statistics. As the US Department of Commerce reported, "Between December 1998 and September 2001, Internet use by individuals in the lowest-income households (those earning less than $15,000 a year) increased at a 25 percent annual growth rate." This meant that poor people were adopting the Internet at an accelerating pace, and faster than upper-income people (most of whom were already online). The same was true of people with little education—and the gender gap had completely disappeared. Thus it looked as if market forces were on their way to solving the Digital Divide, as companies competed to offer cheaper and more attractive services to broader markets. Whereas the US Commerce Department's 1999 report on Internet use was called "Falling Through the Net," the 2002 report was entitled "A Nation Online."

But there are several reasons to continue worrying about equity. First, some of the rapid increases reported in 1998–2002 resulted from federal programs, such as the E-Rate, that are now threatened with termination. This becomes clear when we calculate the importance of Internet access via schools and libraries (which are subsidized by the federal government) for low-income people. For example, there is only a 12 percent difference in computer use between the poorest and richest children, but that is because the low-income students are using computers in schools. There is almost a 60 percent gap in the use of *home* computers between the richest and poorest categories of students. Likewise, African Americans of all ages are more likely (by 10 percentage points) than whites to use the Internet in a public library— because they are less likely to have Internet connections at home. If federal subsidies for library and school computers disappear, then the Digital Divide will quickly reopen.

Moreover, using the Internet from a school or library is not fully satisfactory. Users' time may be limited and there may be rules about what they can do. It is certainly difficult to operate one's own Web site from a library or to learn how software works by playing with the basic settings of a public computer. Internet access from a workplace is often even less satisfactory, since an employer may ban private, social, and political uses outright.

Third, I cannot believe that the rapid rate of Internet adoption among low-income people will continue until the whole population is online. More than 20 percent of American adults are in the lowest literacy category, which means that they cannot enter information on an application for a Social Security card or calculate total costs on an order form. They are not going to be able to make much use of a home computer.

Fourth, the perceived need to get a home computer may be putting severe strains on low-income families. Many parents fear that they will damage their children's prospects if they fail to have an Internet connection at home. In 2001, the *New York Times* reported from a troubled block in Harlem that "some impoverished mothers here, terrified by [the education] gap, have begun leasing computers for their children." This means that poor families are able to overcome the Digital Divide, but only at the cost of other important goals. And they may not be able to keep up.

Finally, wealthy households are much more likely than poor ones to go online via cable lines and other high-speed, "broadband" connections. This gap doesn't matter too much as long as most of the Internet still consists of text and static images. But as broadband becomes more common, more Web sites and even e-mail messages will have elaborate moving pictures. And then low-income people will have to confront a whole new Digital Divide. Indeed, one can see a historical pattern in which new technologies are first adopted by wealthier and better educated people; they become cheaper and more widespread; life without them becomes actively unpleasant because major institutions depend on them; they cease to confer any relative advantages; and then new technologies come along to replace (or at least supplement) them.

None of this necessarily implies that the federal government should directly subsidize home computers and Internet connections until the Digital Divide vanishes. For one thing, such a subsidy would determine the budget priorities for its purported beneficiaries. They would get Internet access instead of (say) car repairs, which they might need more. In my opinion, it is better to expand flexible income support through mechanisms like the Earned Income Tax Credit than to provide targeted subsidies for goods like Internet access. To be sure, society as a whole would benefit if everyone could go online, because (for example) government agencies could eliminate paper forms. But genuine 100 percent Internet usage might well prove impossible.

Thus I am not arguing for any specific government policy regarding the Digital Divide. I am saying that inequity remains a problem, and it is directly relevant to civil society. Although wealthy people may find that civil society becomes more exciting and inviting as it exploits the power of computer networks, poorer and less educated people will have no alternative but to use old-fashioned, face-to-face, local modes of association. Worse, groups that used to include a broad range of people may adopt the Internet and shed their poorer members.

These problems of equity in industrialized countries are easy compared to the situation in the global South. Perhaps computer networks will ultimately strengthen international civil society as well as the array of independent associations within every nation. But the Internet hardly exists in most parts of the world. According to the United Nations Development Programme, in 1999 the industrial nations are home to 15 percent of global population and 88 percent of Internet users. In Africa, just half of one percent of the population is online. A quarter of all the world's countries have less than one telephone for every 100 people, which makes widespread Internet access look hopeless in the near run.

Thin Social Bonds

Some observers fear that the Internet replaces robust, durable, and emotionally satisfying social bonds with superficial and contingent ones. People will not generally develop strong bonds of trust and mutual obligation if computers become their main means of communication. They may communicate more than ever, but when they find themselves in need, they may have no one to turn to.

This prediction is not supported by national surveys of Internet users. The 1996 National Election Study in the US revealed that they had *more* offline or real-world memberships than other people had, and that they were *more* trusting. These generalizations held true even if one compared only people of similar education and income.

Similarly, a survey conducted by UCLA in 2000 found that people who used the Internet spent slightly more time participating in clubs and organizations than people who had never used computer networks; Internet users were also less likely to describe themselves as "lonely." And a 2001 survey by the Pew Internet and American Life Project found that users of the Internet were considerably more likely than nonusers to know their neighbors' names and to belong to various kinds of associations.

In short, people who use the Internet are more active participants in civil society than those who don't go online. But this correlation does not prove that Internet use boosts civic engagement. It could be something else about Internet users that makes them participate in groups: if not their income and education, then their age, their energy, their family status, or their general receptivity to current trends. These people are early adopters of a technology that is still not used by half the population; whatever personal characteristics put them ahead of the line for Internet access may also involve them in offline groups.

It is therefore essential to test the effects of Internet use on a random population over time. In 1998, the Carnegie Mellon HomeNet study found that Pittsburgh residents who were given Internet access began to communicate somewhat less with other members of their own households, and their social networks narrowed. The HomeNet researchers hypothesized that the "time that people devote to using the Internet might substitute for time that they had previously spent engaged in social activities" and that "people are substituting poorer quality social relationships [on the Internet] for better relationships, that is, substituting weak ties for strong ones." Participants also reported an increase in depression as they used the Internet. This study was widely criticized for (among other reasons) failing to identify a control group of Pittsburgh residents without Internet access. But a subsequent experiment by the Stanford Institute for the Quantitative Study of Society generated similar findings. The Institute gave 35,000 people a simple Internet link called "Web-TV" for the first time. They found that new Internet users began spending less time with family and friends and less time attending events outside the home; they also read newspapers less.

If we put these two experiments together with the 1996 data from the National Election Survey, we can generate a tentative hypothesis. People who use the Internet at any date will be more socially connected than those who do not go online—in part because they are better off; in part because their friends in civic and social networks have persuaded them to get connected to the Internet; and in part because they are comparatively active, energetic, and optimistic people who both adopt new technologies and involve themselves in their communities. Yet there is very little civic or social benefit from *Internet use itself.* Indeed, over time a whole society may grow more disengaged or atomistic as a result of using computer networks.

One major reason is anonymity—and the psychological distance, mistrust, and irresponsibility that it often produces. Anonymity is not an inevitable feature of computer networks. I sit at my computer for hours every day. I spend much of this time reading e-mail messages from people I know well, and writing back to them. A company or a government agency can require its clients to disclose their real identities over the Internet, to prove who they are with something like a credit card number, and then to live up to their contractual agreements. What the Internet adds is a new layer of interactions (especially in chat rooms, listservs, and game environments) in which participants withhold practically all information about themselves, including their real names, appearances, demographic characteristics, and locations. They can also break off contact at will, adapt multiple personalities and identities, and shield themselves from the consequences of what they say. Perhaps the same effect could have been achieved one hundred years ago through an elaborate system of anonymous mailboxes, but only at great cost and inconvenience. Widespread anonymity is a new phenomenon, and deeply attractive to at least some of us.

Anonymity, the difficulty of punishing antisocial behavior, the absence of social cues, and the use of temporary, alternative personalities—all these features of typical online interactions weaken social inhibitions and encourage offensive or hostile behavior. (An example is "flaming," or responding to another's communication with extravagant harshness and abuse.)

But it would be wrong to jump to the conclusion that such disengagement is a bad thing. Being able to withhold information about oneself on the Internet sometimes means that one can operate in a race- and gender-blind arena, safe from discrimination. For instance, the city of Santa Monica, California, has given citizens access to a local e-mail network called PEN, with free terminals in public spaces. As a result, homeless residents—previously scorned—have become active participants in creating the city's homelessness policy. On their advice, Santa Monica has begun providing free showers, washers, and lockers. One citizen, Donald Paschal, has written:

> I am homeless. . . .We without shelter are looked on with disdain, fear, loathing, pity, and hatred. This difference makes "normal" contact with other humans almost impossible. Not only might we be dirty, or perhaps smell bad, we are different. In the minds of many, people who are different must be avoided. This is why Santa Monica's PEN system is so special to me. No one on PEN knew that I was homeless until I told them. After I told them, I was still treated like a human being. To me, the most remarkable thing about the PEN community is that a city councilmember and a pauper can coexist, albeit not always in perfect harmony, but on an equal basis. I have met, become friends with, or perhaps adversaries with, people I would otherwise not know of.

This is an inspiring story, but it requires a caveat. Donald Paschal is evidently a skilled writer, so he must be educated (even if he is a successful autodidact). Differences in education, native language, dialect, and sometimes gender remain palpable—even online.

Still, the possibility of remaining partially anonymous may cultivate community by encouraging candor and personal disclosure, especially of shared stigmas. The HomeNet and Stanford Studies have suggested that—in general—citizens will become more isolated as a result of Internet use. But there can be important exceptions. The Internet has put people in touch with others who share rare conditions, beliefs, or dilemmas, thereby allowing them to form significant psychological bonds. Information Systems professor Jenny Preece argues that "empathic communities" are created online by people who share medical problems. She finds evidence of information-sharing and a high degree of emotional support. Sometimes communities are deeper when we can choose our partners, rather than being stuck in the local networks of our birth.

Even if online communities are generally weaker than ones in the real world, this can be an advantage. Because it offers choice, the Internet can provide welcome relief from a repressive world of family, neighborhood, school, and church, which is often rife with oppressive politics.

Political scientist Bruce Bimber's distinction between "thick" and "thin" communities is relevant here. People join "thin" communities because they already possess common beliefs, values, or ends, and they think that they can gain strategic benefits by collaborating. For instance, I may sign up for an e-mail list because I predict that the benefits (information about a specific subject) will outweigh the costs (a cluttered inbox). Later, out of a sense of obligation, I might also contribute information. But I will probably quit as soon as I decide that the overall costs of participating outweigh the benefits. Thus, if we can call the listserv a "community," it is a highly instrumental one. It does require some mutual trust, but the members' confidence in each other can be conditional and limited. In a "thick" community, by contrast, members are committed to the inherent value of the group, to the other participants as partners, and to the ends or values that they decide on collectively. Religions, neighborhoods, and families are often "thick." It is hard to imagine a "thick" community forming online without any presence in the real world. To be sure, committed participants in e-mail, bulletin boards, and online role-playing games *testify* that communities exist online, and that they belong to them. But their reports should not be accepted at face value, because they may lack experience with "thicker" groups.

In liberal societies, citizens have a right to escape from private associations, such as unions, political parties, churches, fraternal organizations, and even families. Ease of exit promotes individual freedom and is preferable (*ceteris paribus*) to the kind of oppression that arises within organizations that control their members by preventing defections. But the genius of civil society is to combine the liberal right of exit with a diverse array of strong, disciplined, "thick" associations. For instance, one can quit a traditional labor union or family, but only at a cost. And one can only enter such groups if one agrees to contribute and to conform to specified norms. By threatening to exclude or expel members, such organizations gain the power to discipline individuals, even in a liberal state.

Disciplined organizations may discriminate against outsiders and oppress people at the bottom of their internal hierarchies. On the other hand, they require their members' *general* assent, and in return they offer political power and paths for advancement. Thus, for instance, a white, working-class American man of the 1950s could count on fairly loyal service from the Democratic Party, the Catholic Church, and labor unions. He could also imagine rising to be a party elder, a cardinal, or a union president. All of these associations have lost membership and political importance, partly as a result of reforms designed to ease entry and exit. For the most part, today's disciplined and powerful organizations are corporations, which offer little to people without skills or wealth. While the voluntary sector has become less discriminatory since the 1950s, it has also grown weaker as a whole, leaving working-class citizens without an important source of power.

The Internet is likely to exacerbate this trend. To join a newsgroup or an e-mail list or to frequent a Web site, one usually clicks a link or two; and to quit is just as simple. Elizabeth Reid observes that "users who engage in disruptive behavior online can be subjected to public rituals intended to humiliate and punish them." But these sanctions are surely weaker online than they would be in the real world. Since Internet groups—with their easy admission and penalty-free exit—cannot effectively discipline their members, they cannot overcome collective-action problems. They lack the means to compel people to serve one another, to deliberate about a common good, or to make sacrifices for that good. Since they cannot harness the resources of individual members, Internet groups can acquire little power in the broader society.

Some enthusiasts think that network technology will allow people to overcome collective-action problems *without* having to subject themselves to hierarchy. They claim that we no longer need either authority or markets to achieve common ends, because we have entered the era of SPINs: "segmented, polycentric, ideologically integrated networks." SPINs are a type of libertarian commons, highly compatible with an open computer network. They include the women's movement of the 1970s, the Zapatistas' supporters in Mexico, the international network of neo-Nazis, and the antiglobalization movement. These networks do not pay or coerce individuals to contribute; instead they use technology to reduce transaction costs and shared values to motivate their members. "The information revolution favors and strengthens networks, while it erodes hierarchies," we are told. But devising and implementing a positive program almost certainly requires collective decision making and discipline. While the antiglobalization movement can put protesters on the street, I doubt that it will create a new system of international trade. And if one of its undisciplined members commits an atrocity, the movement will die.

Threats to Public Deliberation Online

Apart from human bonds and trust, another good that people expect from civil society is public deliberation. Popular opinion is supposed to guide—or at least constrain—democratic governments. But people do not automatically possess conscious views and opinions about major public issues. Citizens acquire these opinions by participating in or observing discussions, either written or oral. Their opinions can be wise or foolish, selfish or altruistic. But deliberation is the most democratic way to *improve* citizens' views. Without imposing a conclusion on anyone, deliberation forces individuals to defend their proposals before others who may have different interests, backgrounds, and information. As a result, overtly selfish or foolish ideas tend to drop out. Finally, deliberation is an essential means of a communication between the public and the government. Decision-makers cannot use election results alone to ascertain what the public wants, because the meaning of a vote is always ambiguous. Except by listening and talking, leaders will not be able to learn their constituents' values and priorities.

The Internet is home to discussion groups, mailing lists, blogs (Web logs), and chat sessions devoted to every conceivable subject, so the sheer quantity of political talk is likely to increase as a result of its growth. But the *quality* of public discussion may worsen, because the Internet gives users the capacity to filter communication. In traditional media, we have limited control over the ideas that we encounter. Consider, for instance, someone who subscribes to a newspaper because he wants specialized information relevant to his own career, his favorite sports team, or his local community. Or perhaps he enjoys having his views reinforced by congenial editorials. As he leafs through a general-interest newspaper, he cannot help stumbling across novel ideas, alien perspectives, and upsetting information about *other people's* lives. Internet users can avoid all this trouble. They can search for just the information and ideas they want, remaining safely in the company of people with similar views and interests. Even those who subscribe to very unusual ideologies will be able to find others from around the world who have identical beliefs. Selective reading is probably almost as old as writing itself, and is a perfectly reasonable way of dealing with excessive quantities of information. But the search functions available on the Internet make selection too easy and threaten to tip the balance toward hyperspecialization.

Information scholars Marshall van Alstyne and Erik Brynjolfsson have devised an elegant proof for the proposition that "connectivity"—the ability to communicate quickly and cheaply with many people—encourages "balkanization," defined as a proliferation of separate communities or conversations that are not in mutual contact. Balkanization results if individuals can choose their partners freely from among larger populations, if each person has a finite capacity to absorb information, and if most people have at least mild preferences for specific types of ideas and facts. A similar logic suggests that the Internet may increase intellectual *stratification* as experts are able to talk only among themselves and can refuse contacts with laypeople.

The general trend in American culture is away from diverse, multipurpose organizations (such as unions, national churches, and strong geographical communities), toward single-interest associations with narrow niches. Local organizations that used to draw people from different occupations, such as the Masons and the PTA, have lost most of their members, while national organizations for people in particular fields or with particular interests have grown. Between 1972 and 1992, Americans became considerably less likely to belong to groups, attend meetings, read newspapers, or express interest in politics—all measures of their general willingness to interact with those different from themselves.

Two of the basic technologies of the World Wide Web—hypertext and search functions—assist users in filtering what they see and hear. These are supposed to be liberating technologies, because users make their own decisions about what to look at next, which thread to follow, and when to move on. But true freedom means being able to follow *someone else's* train of thought for a while. One can escape from one's own preconceptions only by following a sustained argument, a plot line, a pattern of allusion, or a meticulous interpretation. That is why reading a whole book can be extraordinarily liberating. There are plenty of books online, including the complete works of Plato and Shakespeare. But we cannot experience Platonic arguments or Shakespearean characters by looking for keywords and clicking our way quickly across the World Wide Web.

Private filtering can have harmful social consequences. Imagine if a person is uninterested in environmental issues and generally unwilling to learn about them. But if she had read about the value of recycling in a general-interest newspaper (or seen a national television broadcast on the subject), then she would have recycled. Since today she can obtain her news from the Internet without having to deal with proenvironmental arguments and evidence, she drops her newspaper subscription and never learns the value of recycling. The Internet is partly at fault.

Further, the Internet provides few effective ways for people to put their case to others who are not initially disposed to listen. Journalist and lawyer Andrew Shapiro argues that Web users are unlike visitors to a physical space, because they do "not have to hear the civil rights marcher, take a leaflet from the striking worker, or see the unwashed homeless person. Their world [can] be cleansed of all interactions save those they explicitly [choose]." A similar logic suggests that the Internet may increase intellectual *stratification* as experts are able to talk only among themselves and ignore the rest of the public.

Cass Sunstein, a political and legal theorist who has done much to advance our understanding of deliberation, summarizes the disadvantages of balkanization in his book *Republic.com.* Among other problems, balkanized groups tend to move toward the views of their own most radical members. Members of such groups do not understand other perspectives or learn how to relate to people who are different. Not realizing that some thoughtful citizens disagree with them, they assume that the government is corrupt when it takes contrary positions. And they constantly reinforce their own beliefs—even completely false ones—without ever being challenged. For instance, many people who are opposed to gun control have encountered the following quotation more than once online: "This year will go down in history! For the first time, a civilized nation has full gun registration! Our streets will be safer, our police more efficient, and the world will follow our lead into the future!" On numerous Web sites, this quote is attributed to Adolf Hitler, who is supposed to have extolled gun control in the *Berlin Daily* on April 15, 1935 (page 3, article 2). Everything about this alleged statement is false, including the implication that the Nazi government imposed gun control. But only Second Amendment purists are likely to encounter it, and their faith is never challenged.

Another danger is that "thin" online groups won't foster deliberation as much as "thick" traditional ones have. Recall that people join "thin" groups because they already share ends or values. Dennis Thompson lists some examples that he has found on the Internet: "Hikers to Free our Parks, National Whistleblower Union, Citizens against Daylight Savings Time, Citizens for Finnish-American Power, the US Committee to Support the Revolution in Peru, and the Anarchists Anti-Defamation League." Members of these groups probably spend little time debating their core values or purposes, which are fixed from the beginning. We might hope that opposing "thin" groups would debate *one another*, but this may not happen on the Internet, because individuals can filter out anything that they don't want to hear. There is no common space, mass audience, or means of addressing people who don't seek out the speaker.

In a "thick" community, on the other hand, the members' commitment is to the group itself, although its purposes and values may be undecided. Unless the group is authoritarian, its members will have to debate their common ends, thus contributing to public deliberation. But "thick" organizations are rare online.

A related issue is social scientist Albert O. Hirschman's contrast between "voice" and "exit." Except in highly coercive organizations (such as some military units and authoritarian states), people who are not fully satisfied with their groups may choose between two strategies. Exercising their "voice," they may complain, seek change, and cultivate support among fellow members. Alternatively, they can leave the association, perhaps to join a different one. People typically follow the path of least resistance. For example, if the only way to exit a democratic state is to emigrate, but speech is constitutionally protected, then citizens typically use voice. On the other hand, if firms in a competitive labor market do not respond to employees' complaints, then disgruntled workers tend to exit.

Both voice and exit promise social benefits. By exiting, group members can reduce the size of their own organizations and enlarge other, more desirable ones. In short, competition is the means by which exit generates progress. Voice works more directly, as group members deliberate about how to improve their associations. It seems likely that exit prevails over voice—and competition over deliberation—on the Internet. It is very easy to leave any Internet-based group, but it is difficult to change the prevailing norms within such groups, because there is no means of enforcing agreements. The result may be a decrease in the total amount of public deliberation, especially about ends and values.

Consumer Choice

The ethos of the Internet is consumer choice. Daily, the business section of any American newspaper informs readers that computer networks will help consumers find goods more quickly and cheaply than previously imaginable. Likewise, one can easily find the religious community, support group, or political lobby that most closely fits one's preferences.

Consumer choice has value; it is certainly preferable to despotism. But there are several reasons to worry about rampant consumerism from a civic point of view.

First, consumption is often considered less dignified and valuable than production and creativity. The Catholic Church teaches: "Work is a good thing for man—a good thing for his humanity—because through work man not only transforms nature, adapting it to his own needs, but he also achieves fulfillment as a human being and indeed in a sense becomes 'more a human being'." In a similar vein, Hannah Arendt argued for the fundamental importance of creative activity that produced lasting objects of value—"work"—and also deliberation and cooperation among human beings: "action." When people describe activities as "civic," or as the proper tasks of citizens, they usually have Arendt's "work" in mind. Thus, for instance, Harry Boyte wants to push the concepts of civil society and democracy "off the playground." He contends that "democracy is not mainly a set of institutions but rather a work in progress in which people continuously create and recreate public things of many sorts (including public institutions)."

The initial promise of the Internet was its capacity to make everyone into a publisher, an artist, or a software engineer. But the percentage of Internet users who *create* material has fallen dramatically. The Stanford researchers found that, "for the most part, the Internet today is a giant public library with a decidedly commercial tilt. The most widespread use of the Internet today is as an information search utility for products, travel, hobbies, and general information. Virtually all users interviewed responded that they engaged in one or more of these information gathering activities." If the Internet makes consumption easier but does not encourage many people to create goods—and especially not free or public goods—then it will do net harm to civil society.

Second, consumer choice is not the same as freedom. To choose what you want to see or buy based on your own preferences is not evidence of autonomy, because your preferences may have been formed without reflection or an awareness of alternatives. Someone who spends his Sunday at the shopping mall buying whatever he wants is not free if no one has ever made a serious case that he ought to spend his time in a church, a forest, or a political campaign. The Internet's potential for filtering reduces the chance that people will be exposed to such arguments.

Some enthusiasts imagine a near future in which all of our communications devices—our television sets and car radios as well as our computers—will be attached to the Internet through wireless connections. Every time we choose to watch or hear or buy something, computers will record this information in order to determine our preferences. We will then receive advertising that is tailored specifically to our preference profiles. Advertisers will save money, because they "don't want to pay to deliver ads to people who have no interest in their products." There will also be savings for consumers, who will "receive information that is timely and relevant" and avoid "the clutter of unwanted ads and solicitations." Indeed, if the targeting works, then we will desire almost *everything* that we see advertised, rather than a small fraction of it. We will recognize many unfilled needs and wants that might otherwise have escaped our notice. We will thus find ourselves walking on an endless treadmill of unfulfilled desire. This seems to me a frightening image of heteronomy, since we will be slaves to our own past preferences. Furthermore, no one will send targeted messages asking consumers to be more active in their communities, more concerned about future generations, more charitable, or better informed about public affairs. Already, as Andrew Shapiro notes, "there are endless newsgroups, e-mail lists, and other online information sources dedicated to the most specific interests, but you'd be hard pressed to find a [group] committed to the General Common Good." The share of time and money that we spend on civic activities may thus fall as a result of more efficient commercial advertising.

A third problem is that consumer choice is a poor way to understand freedom of *expression*. We are free to express ourselves when we can address chosen audiences with uncensored messages. This freedom must always be limited, because otherwise an individual could monopolize public spaces, take over private forums, or harass other citizens with unwanted and persistent messages. There is often a tension between the right to express oneself freely to anyone and the right to decide what one hears and sees. But in a regime of pure consumer choice, the freedom to address others would vanish, since each person would be completely free to choose what messages to receive (messages being viewed as consumer products). This is the general trend on the Internet. In the real world, one can hand out leaflets at a street corner or picket a company's headquarters, but individuals have no means to address people who surf past a given Web site (unless they happen to own it).

More generally, consumer choice is not the only way to express preferences. We select commodities in the market, but we also choose occupations, friends, companions, and political leaders. The logic of these other choices is formally different from that of consumer behavior. For instance, when I support a policy or ideology by casting a vote, I hope that my decision will bind everyone, whereas when I choose a product in the supermarket, I can only express a personal inclination. Similarly, when I select a consumer product, I assume none of the obligations that come with initiating a personal relationship. The roles of consumers, voters, workers, and companions are different, and they require distinct sets of skills and attitudes. In a culture of rampant consumerism, we could lose our capacity to make these other choices wisely.

A final problem is the incompatibility of consumer choice with alternative cultural norms and values. To mention just one example, Islam is not viewed by its adherents as a choice that may happen to fit some individuals' preferences and that comes in various flavors for various tastes. It means "submission": obedience to the authority of God. True enough, people anywhere in the world can now "discover Islam" through www.islamonline.net and myriad other Moslem Web sites. They can download translations of the Koran, search databases of *fatwas*, and receive instructions from Islamic "cybercounselors." For people who are already committed to Islam, computer networks may prove useful. But inevitably the Internet makes Islam look like a choice, something that one can opt to do instead of (or in addition to) reading about environmentalism, following an athletic team, or looking at naked models. The "islamonline" site is just a few clicks away from any of these alternatives. In a wired world, Islam will have to compete directly for individuals' attention, and will not be able to count on tradition or authority to steer believers to the right sites and the right beliefs.

A survey of Americans who visited selected Christian Web sites found that for the most part they were seeking thoughts, advice, and stories that they could put together to make a congenial religious package of their own devising. "Organizational loyalty and connections are not the driving force behind people's interest in getting information about religion from the Internet. Rather [users] want information that will assist them in determining not only how they will respond to institutions but how they will take individual actions." In other words, Americans are using the Internet to treat religions as they would treat consumer goods.

The conflict between private consumer choice and deep cultural or spiritual commitments is not easy to resolve. If pressed, I would favor consumer choice, but I would also regret the inevitable losses. Apart from anything else, the Internet may decrease the *pluralism* of civil society, even though it is often touted as a source of diversity. After all, some cultures are incompatible with free individual consumption.

Privacy

Civil society requires a particular degree and type of privacy. In public institutions such as courts and legislatures, all business is normally supposed to be public and transparent. In intimate matters such as health, sexuality, and parenthood, privacy is the norm. But in civil society, citizens make selective disclosures of personal information within groups. For instance, members of civic associations exchange opinions about social issues without necessarily disclosing these views to outsiders. Neighbors observe one another shopping and gardening, but do not know how the people next door behave in their bedrooms or in the voting booth.

The Internet changes the nature and limits of privacy. On one hand, it allows us to conceal facts about our appearance, gender, age, and race from other individuals with whom we communicate. This potential increase in privacy has its advantages, but it may weaken intimate horizontal bonds: that is, relationships among citizens as equals. On the other hand, the owners of computer networks can acquire and sell information about all the individuals who use their services. Computers can monitor what people say and to whom, what sites they visit online, and what they buy and sell. What's more, computers can aggregate this information, turning a mere list of purchases into a consumer profile and then adding information from public records. For instance, a company called Aristotle International has built a database of 150 million Americans. According to the *New York Times*,

> Drawing on state motor vehicle registrations, the Postal Service and Census Bureau, among other sources, the Aristotle databank includes a person's age, sex, telephone number, party affiliation and estimated income, whether he or she rents or owns a home, has children, and has an ethnic surname. It also provides the make and model of voters' cars, whether they are campaign donors, their employer and occupation, and how often they vote.

Individuals can be defamed when the information in such databases is false or is portrayed in a misleading light. Even accurate data can be used to discriminate against employees in morally objectionable ways. Databases may also violate property rights, since a person's "profile" arguably belongs to her. An erosion of privacy may prevent people from developing complex personalities, because maturity requires trying out ideas and personas in private. And citizens may simply be made less *happy* as a result of losing their privacy.

Such databases may not only damage personal happiness and freedom, but also undermine the importance of *voluntary association* by forcing us to make public what we would prefer to disclose only to fellow members of a group. And since information about people is a source of power, citizens who lose the effective right to withhold information will become weaker compared to governments and large organizations.

Conclusion

The purpose of this article has not been to issue dire predictions about the probable effects of the Internet on civil society. The Internet may prove beneficial to civil life. Rather, this article identified some potential problems that we can still solve. The Internet need not be left alone to develop haphazardly. Law can protect such values as personal privacy. The contexts in which the Internet is used (especially schools and public libraries) can be managed to assure that computers serve public purposes. Children can be taught to use networks critically and for civic purposes. One especially promising suggestion for reform is the idea of new online public spaces that would be reserved for civic uses and subsidized by the state. In short, the Internet cannot be faulted if civil society is irreparably weakened—*we* will deserve the blame for our failure to act.

This chapter was based on an earlier work in *The Report from the Institute for Philosophy and Public Policy,* volume 20, fall 2000.

Sources

See Pew Research Center for the People and the Press, *The Internet Audience Goes Ordinary* (1999; see www.peoplepress.org/ tech98sum.htm); US Department of Commerce, National Telecommunications & Information Administration (NTIA), *Falling*

Through the Net: Defining the Digital Divide (1999; see www. ntia.doc.gov/ntiahome/fttn99/contents.html); Stanford Institute for the Quantitative Study of Society, *Internet Study* (2000; www. stanford.edu/group/siqss/ Press_Release/internetStudy.html); and NTIA, *A Nation Online: How Americans are Expanding their Use of the Internet* (February 2002); Leslie Harris and Associates, "Bring a Nation Online: The Importance of Federal Leadership" (July 2002), available via www.benton.org; Department of Education's National Adult Literacy Survey (NALS); see http://www. nifl.gov/reders/reder.htm. Already in 1999, 43 percent of American parents polled by the Annenberg Public Policy Center agreed: "Children who do not have Internet access are at a disadvantage compared to peers. . . ." Joseph Turow, *The Internet and the Family: The View from Parents, The View from the Press* (Philadelphia: Annenberg, 1999); Amy Waldman, "An American Block: Life on 129th Street," *New York Times* (February 19, 2001); U.N. Development Programme, *Human Development Report* (Oxford: Oxford University Press, 1999). For an earlier essay on social bonds and deliberation online, see D. C. Seyle, "Dot-Com Democracy: Computer-Mediated Communication, Community, and Delibera-tion" (2000) and available from the Kettering Foundation at www.kettering.org. Of Internet users, 49.3 percent said that they trusted most people most of the time; 91.7 percent said that they were members of at least one group; and 71.3 percent said that they belonged to at least two groups. By contrast, of non-Internet-users, only 33.1 percent said that they trusted most people most of the time; 80.3 percent said that they were members of at least one group; and 54.6 percent belonged to two or more groups. These correlations generally remained valid even if one controlled for education and income. One exception: even though both educa-tion and Internet access correlated with trust, people who had at least seventeen years of formal schooling and lacked Internet access appeared to be *more* trusting than similarly educated people who used the Internet. This according to NES data, available via csa.berkeley.edu:7502/archive.htm. J. I. Cole, *The UCLA Internet Report: Surveying the Digital Future* (2000; see www.ccp. ucla.edu/pages/internet-report.asp). The UCLA survey also con-tained some negative findings. Internet users said that they spent less time than others socializing with household members. They valued civic goals—such as volunteering and protecting the envi-ronment—less than other people did (while they put a higher pri-ority on "making a lot of money"). And they had less trust for edu-cation. However, these results were not controlled for age, educa-tion, gender, or income. Pew Internet and American Life Project, Online Communities Survey (2001), available from www. pewinternet.org. Kraut, V. Lundmark, M. Patterson, S. Kiesler, T.

Mukopadhyay, and W. Scherlis, "A social technology that reduces social involvement and psychological well-being?" *American Psychologist*, vol. 53 (1998). The UCLA survey (see Cole, 2000) asked people to assess the effect of the Internet on their own social connections over time. On average, respondents felt that computers had increased their contact with family and friends and with professional colleagues, while decreasing their contact with coreligionists and with people who shared their political beliefs. They thought that their contacts with people who shared their recreational interests had increased, but very slightly. I think, however, that such retrospective self-reports should be viewed with utmost skepticism. J. Van Tassel, "Yakety-Yak, Do Talk Back! PEN, The Nation's First Publicly Funded Electronic Network, Makes a Difference in Santa Monica," *Wired*, 2.01 (1994). A. Joinson, "Causes and Implications of Disinhibited Behavior on the Internet," in J. Gackenbach, ed., *Psychology and the Internet: Intrapersonal, Interpersonal, and Transpersonal Implications* (San Diego: Academic Press, 1998); J. Preece, "Empathetic Communities: Reaching Out Across the Web," *ACM Interactions*, vol. 5 (1998). The quote that the Internet can provide release from "the repressive world . . . " is from M. Friedman, "Feminism and Modern Friendship: Dislocating the Community," *Ethics*, vol. 99 (1989), p. 281; B. Bimber, "The Internet and Political Transformation: Populism, Community, and Accelerated Pluralism," *Polity*, vol. 31 (1998); C. Haythorthwaite, B. Wellman, and L. Garton, "Work and Community Via Computer-Mediated Communications" (1998), in Gackenbach, ed.; E. Reid, "The Self and the Internet: Variations of the Illusion of One Self," in Gackenbach, ed.; J. Arquilla and D. Ronfeldt, "The Advent of Netwar," in *Athena's Camp: Preparing for Conflict in the Information Age*, edited by Arquilla and Ronfeldt (Santa Monica, CA: RAND, 1999). For a further discussion of leaders listening and talking constituents to learn of their values and priorities, see: Peter Levine, *The New Progressive Era: Toward a Fair and Deliberative Democracy* (Rowman & Littlefield, 2000); A. L. Shapiro, *The Control Revolution* (New York: Century Foundation/Public Affairs, 1999); M. Van Alstyne and E. Brynjolfssin, "Electronic Communities: Global Village or Cyberbalkans?" (1997; see web.mit.edu/marshall/www/papers/CyberBalkans.pdf); see www.urbanlegends.com/politics/hitler_gun_control.html; D. Thompson, "E-mail from James Madison re: Cyberdemocracy," in *Democracy.com? Governance in a Networked World*, edited by E. C. Kamarck and J. S. Nye (Hollis, MD: Hollis Publishing, 1999); A. O. Hirschman, *Exit, Voice, and Loyalty* (Cambridge, MA: Harvard University Press, 1971); John Paul II, *On Human Work* (Laborem exercens), 1981, §29, §40; H. Arendt, *The Human Condition* (Chicago: University of Chicago Press, 1958); H. C. Boyte, "Off the Playground of Civil Society," *The Good Society*, vol. 9

(1999); K. O'Connor, "The High Cost of Net Privacy," *Wall Street Journal* (March 7, 2000); K. Bedell, "The Extent and Nature of Religion on the Internet: A Report on a Ten Month Visit to the World of the Internet." For United Methodist Communication and the Louisville Institute (1998; see www.religion-research.org/report1.htm); H. Nissenbaum, "Protecting Privacy in an Information Age: The Problem of Privacy in Public," *Law and Philosophy*, vol. 17 (1998); L. Wayne, "Voter Profiles Selling Briskly as Privacy Issues are Raised," *New York Times* (September 9, 2000).

Social Capital and the Net

Eric M. Uslaner

A century and a half ago the French journalist Alexis de Tocqueville travelled throughout the United States and marvelled at the generosity of the American people. "When an American asks for the co-operation of his fellow citizens, it is seldom refused; and I have often seen it afforded spontaneously, and with great goodwill," Tocqueville argued. He attributed this generosity to the Americans' tendency to look beyond their own immediate concerns: "The principle of self-interest rightly understood produces no great acts of self-sacrifice, but it suggests daily small acts of self-denial. . . . If the principle of interest rightly understood were to sway the whole moral world, extraordinary virtues would doubtless be more rare." This idea of self-interest rightly understood we now call trust in other people. According to Tocqueville and many who have followed in his footsteps, people develop trust in each other when they join together for common purposes in civic associations. Indeed, political theorist Robert Putnam referred to a "virtuous circle" of trust, group membership, and informal social ties that has become known as "social capital." Social capital helps make society and its government run more smoothly.

Yet, beginning in the late 1960s and early 1970s, this circle somehow broke. Americans began to withdraw from participation in all sorts of civic groups—from the traditional service organizations such as the Rotary Clubs, Kiwanis, and the League of Women Voters as well as bowling leagues and card-playing clubs. We socialized less with friends and neighbors and we voted less often. The inevitable result was that we became less trusting of one another. In 1960, 58 percent of Americans believed that "most people can be trusted" (as opposed to saying that "you can't be too careful in dealing with people"). By 2003 barely more than a third of Americans trusted each other, according to national surveys such as the General Social Survey, the American National Election Study, and the Pew Internet and American Life Center. Americans have lost their sense of community. We don't mix with each other as much as we used to and we don't trust each other. We have become more balkanized, our public life has become more contentious, and our national institutions (especially the Congress), struggle to compromise on even the most basic public policy questions.

The villain in the decline of social capital, Putnam argues, is technology—initially television and now the Internet. Watching a lot of television keeps us inside our homes and away from the civic organizations and social connections that generate trust. Heavy TV viewing also leads us to believe that the real world is as "mean" and violent as the programs we see on television—so it makes us less likely to trust strangers. Television produces misanthropes—who see the world as a dark and threatening place and whose "Friends" are fictional characters whom you will never be asked to help out.

That's the old technology. Today there are even more "mistrusters," and civic engagement has dropped further. The new culprit seems to be the Internet. Even more so than television, the Internet may be a lonely place. We hear stories of people who become addicted to the Net, who spend their hours in front of a computer screen and ignore their families and dissociate themselves from friends. Television programs may make you think that the world is mean. The Internet will show you just how nasty folks can be. When you enter an Internet chat room, you can hide your identity, "flame" other people, and "troll" first-time visitors to a Web site. The Net can be a dangerous place, where "charities" solicit funds for nonexistent causes, scoundrels feign love for lonely hearts, and unscrupulous hackers uncover your credit card numbers. Heavy Internet users *become* more depressed, lead more stressful lives, and have fewer friends—even though they may start out as well off psychologically as the rest of us.

Internet researchers R. Kraut and colleagues, and Norman Nie and Lutz Ebring report that heavy Internet users disclose that they have cut back on their social ties. Net use leads people away from social contacts and toward staring at their monitors in not-so-splendid isolation. The newsmagazine *US News and World Report* published a special investigative report suggesting that "the amount of bad stuff out there is truly staggering"—adoption scams, stalking complaints, rigged auctions, and even "the first Internet serial killer." Yet, this is just one face of the Internet. Others see the Internet as the great opportunity to rebuild our lost sense of community and trust. People come together on the Net through e-mail lists, affinity groups, support groups, and chat rooms. The Internet connects people from all over the world—and may be, as researchers Michael Hauben and Ronda Hauben argue, "a grand intellectual and social commune in the spirit of the collective nature present at the origins of human society." The Internet is the great leveller of class and race barriers—which have proven to be strong barriers to effective participation in American society. As computer literacy and Internet access grow, Americans should reconnect with each other—thus forming the base for a new era of trust. I offer a third perspective: The Internet neither destroys nor creates social capital. There are both altruists and scoundrels on the Net, just as there are in everyday life. Indeed, the Internet, like television, mirrors everyday life. What people do online is pretty much what they do offline: They shop, they get sports news and weather, they plan their vacations, and, most of all, they contact people they already know through e-mail. The Net is not a threat. But it is not Nirvana either.

The major reason why the Internet is not the "new new thing" of trust and civic engagement is that much of the current discussion of the "virtuous circle" of trust, civic engagement, and socializing is misplaced. Trust in other people is trust in strangers, people who are different from yourself. Trust is essential for a civil and a cooperative society, but it does *not* depend upon your life experiences—whether you visit friends and relatives, join civic organizations, watch television, or surf the Internet. Instead, trust reflects an optimistic worldview and a belief that others share your fundamental values. You learn trust from your parents. You are not likely to become more trusting in people who are different from yourself by interacting in clubs or in coffee klatches with people like yourself. Trust is not irrelevant to the Internet. Far from it. Going online does not make people either more or less trusting, but trust shapes how people interact with each other. Trusting people are less likely to fear getting involved with strangers. In everyday life, trusters are less likely to lock their doors at night and to use guns to protect themselves. They are more likely to volunteer and give to charity. On the Net trusting people should see others as nice folks who won't exploit them—so they should be less worried about violations of their privacy and will be more likely to buy goods on the Net. There is little reason to believe that people who trust others will be more or less likely to use the Internet otherwise. What about the other aspects of social capital, civic engagement and sociability? Perhaps people who use the Internet a lot are hermits, but more likely they are sociable. From e-mail (the most widely used part of the Internet) to chat rooms to support groups, going online involves communicating with others.

The Internet is not likely to create the kinds of communities that could generate trust. Trust develops between people of divergent backgrounds, whereas the Net excels in bringing together people who already have something in common—be it family ties, friendship, working in the same office, political views, or needing the same kind of medical information or psychological support. One of the most heralded forms of online communities—the medical support groups—brings together people who may know nothing about each other *except that they share the same malady.* And since many of these conditions are temporary—such as sports injuries—these online communities may well be populated primarily by transients. Nevertheless, simply going online for information and support is hardly the hallmark of a troglodyte.

What the Data Tell Us

What is the connection between trust, sociability, and Internet usage? I analyzed data from a 1998 survey of technology use by the Pew Research Center for the People and the Press. The survey asked 2,000 Americans a variety of questions about going online as well as questions about people's social networks and their trust in others and in government. (Alas, there are no questions on group membership, which is a key element of social capital.) I estimated almost twenty models using a statistical technique called ordered probit analysis. These models allow me to determine which factors best predict different forms of Internet use. Each model contains many factors that might lead to more Internet usage, but I focus on trust and measures of sociability (how wide is your social support network, how often you visit family members, and how frequently you call friends).

Unlike researchers Kraut et al., and Nie and Erbring surveys of people who were given computers so that they would go online, the Pew Center survey is a representative national sample of the population with a much larger number of respondents (2,000 compared to 169). Examining only those people who go online may lead to erroneous conclusions, especially since most people don't spend a lot of time on the Internet. The Internet usage variables fall into four categories: general use of the net, how often people go online, making social connections online, and worries about privacy and security on the net. I summarize the results of the statistical models in table 6-1. And they are telling: The Internet is neither the tool of the devil nor the new Jerusalem—which heralds the renaissance of a national sense of community and trust in one another. For most types of general use of the Internet—using e-mail, getting information on health, business, sports, and stocks, expressing your views online, and buying goods online—trust either doesn't matter at all or not much. Surprisingly, e-mail users are more likely to trust others and people who buy goods online are ever so slightly more likely to trust others. Beyond that, general use of the Internet is connected neither to trust nor to sociability. All sorts of people go online to seek information—the trusting and the misanthrope, the sociable and the recluse. There is little reason to expect that simply going online either taps or drains sociability (or trust).

Kraut et al. and Nie and Erbring argue that people who spend a lot of time online are the misanthropes. But the 1998 Pew Center survey offers little support for this view. People who use their computers a lot, who spent a lot of time online yesterday (both in real time and how often they connected), and who *say that they spend too much time on the Net,* are no less trusting than people who don't go online at all. Neither the Internet nor television remakes people's personalities. And the picture of heavy surfers as loners is also wrong: *The heaviest users of the Internet have wider social circles and support networks.* The Internet, then, does not herald a new spirit of community. Rather, it is an additional outlet for people who already are connected to other people, as others have also found.

The new innovation of the Internet—chat rooms—offers some hope that people of different backgrounds might get together and learn to trust one another. But here, of all places, we see some evidence of misanthropy. People who visit chat rooms or who make new friends online are no more or less sociable than anyone else. They don't have bigger or smaller support networks and are no more like-ly to visit relatives or call friends. Yet, they are *less trusting* than oth-ers. Perhaps people who make friends online, often anonymously, feel uncomfortable with meeting "real" strangers. And many, maybe most, chat rooms are marked by a dominant worldview or ideology—and dissidents often find out rather rudely that they are not welcome. People who frequent chat rooms seem to trust only people like them-selves and fear people with different views.

The Pew Internet and American Life has conducted two further surveys since 1998. The Trust and Privacy Survey in 2000 and the Internet Spam Survey in 2003. The Pew Trust and Privacy Survey in 2000 shows a high level of distrust of strangers: 61 percent say that you can't be too careful in dealing with people. And mistrusters are *very* concerned about the Internet. They see it as a threatening place, where hackers might steal your credit card number, businesses will get personal information, Web dealings will not be private, others will know where you have been on the Web, you might download a virus, and others will learn private things about your life. In turn, they tend to limit their interactions. They don't respond to e-mail from strangers—even though they are *more* likely to say that they have received an offensive e-mail from a stranger. They respond in kind, being *less* likely to use their real name on the Web and *more* likely to use fake identifications and e-mail addresses on the Web.

Trusting people show just the opposite profile. They respond to e-mails from strangers—and receive fewer offensive missives from peo-ple they don't know (either because it takes more to offend them or they get on fewer lists with people who write nasty notes). They worry less about what others might learn about them and don't fear that others will invade their personal lives or spread lies. They are more likely to demand that companies ask permission to get person-al information, but they will use their credit card numbers for phone orders (though, surprisingly, there is no difference for Internet orders). Trusting people overall see the web as a place occupied with lots of trustworthy people and companies. They have no desire to hide their identity.

On matters not related to privacy and security, there is little that separates trusters and mistrusters on the Net. Trusting people are no more likely to go online to get information of any sort—or even to buy products. They are no more prone to go to the Web for fun—or to spend lots of time on it.

Across forty-three questions relating to Internet usage, the only significant differences between trusters and mistrusters is over identity and privacy issues. Mistrusters worry that someone—or some company—is lurking out there, collecting personal information about them. In turn, they adopt a defensive posture: They lie about their own identity more than trusters and give out fake e-mail addresses to their new online "friends." Mistrusters were (at least in 2000) substantially less likely to engage in Internet commerce than trusters, for fear that someone might use their information (credit cards, phone numbers, addresses) to hurt them.

Yet, by 2003, there were no significant differences between trusters and mistrusters on what spam is, how dangerous it is, or whether it can be controlled. The 2003 survey (with 2,200 respondents) once again found a mistrusting country. Spam has become such a widespread problem that trusters and mistrusters alike find that it has made online life annoying. But trusters and mistrusters both continue to say that they will persevere with e-mail communications even in the face of the spam barrage. Mistrusters don't feel that they are being singled out by spam—and they are no less trusting of e-mail in general than are people who believe that "most people can be trusted." It seems as if spam is everywhere and everyone knows it. So there is nothing special about receiving advertisements for Viagra, mortgages, or even pornography. Mistrusters are not even less likely than trusters to order a product offered in an unsolicited e-mail or to have clicked on a link in such an e-mail to get more information. Spam may be the greater leveler of the Internet—but in a negative way. It is making *all* Net users more wary of what is out there in cyberspace.

People who mistrust others fear the Internet much as they accept all sorts of other conspiracy theories that we see on the "X Files." They worry about their privacy generally and in particular about the security of their medical records and downloading viruses. Trusters see the Internet as more benign. Trusting people believe that they can control the world and have faith that science will solve our problems. They see the Internet as an additional tool that gives them leverage over their world.

The Internet, then, is not a reservoir of social capital. As in everyday life, there are places where trust matters and there are even more places where it doesn't. Trust matters most when people fear the unknown and worry that this new technology can come back to haunt them. And there is little evidence that the Internet will create new communities to make up for the decline in civic engagement that has occurred over the past four decades in the United States. Yet, there is even less evidence that the Internet is pushing people away from traditional social ties or making them less trusting. Internet use neither consumes nor produces trust. Neither the number of listservs you belong to, how often you go online, whether you are willing to give your views on political or social issues online, or whether you enter chat rooms makes you more trusting. And *the more people use e-mail, the less trusting they seem to become.* Surfing the Net will not turn a misanthrope into a truster.

The Pew Center surveys do not allow a good test of the effects of Internet use on trust because they do not include most of the factors that I have elsewhere found to be the most important reasons people trust others (a general sense of optimism and control). The 1996 American National Election Survey does permit a rough test of the effect of Internet use on trust. The test is not ideal, because the survey asked only whether people had Internet access, not whether they went online or what sites they visited. And Internet usage was substantially less in 1996 than in the past. But it is the best test available—and it shows just what I would expect: Internet access leads to neither more nor less trust, once we take other factors (such as general optimism, age, and education, among other variables) into account.

Circling the Wagons?

This completes the circle. It is neither vicious nor virtuous. The Internet is neither a dark and threatening place nor is it "a grand intellectual and social commune." Yes, the Internet is filled with pornography, but it didn't invent it and nobody is forcing folks to visit pornography sites (or others that sell Viagra to dogs or let children gamble). And yes, there are more opportunities on the Web to give to charities, to find volunteering opportunities, and to join support groups. But that isn't the whole Internet either. The World Wide Web is very much like the World. It makes things better in some ways and worse in others. But it is not transforming. If you want to make a revolution, you have to go offline.

The message of these findings is the Internet is not a threat to our society or its moral fiber. Regulating the Net won't solve our social problems or save our children from evil influences. Children develop trust in others by learning from—and emulating—their parents, and not from what they (don't) see on television or on the Web. And how much you trust others as a child largely determines how much you trust others as an adult. Yes, the world *may* seem a more dangerous place on television or on the Web. And the Internet makes such mean sites more readily available than the everyday world (or even television). But this does not mean that the net (or any other form of media) poses a real threat to most families. By itself, it is neither a threat to civil society and sociability or its panacea.

This chapter is based on an earlier work, "Social Capital and the Net," in *Communications of the ACM*, vol. 43, no. 12 (December 2000) © Association for Computing Machinery, 2000, http://portal. acm.org/portal.cfm. I am grateful to the Association and to Andrew Rosenbloom for permission to reprint this expanded version. I am also grateful to Ben Shneiderman and Peter Levine of the University of Maryland for sparking my interest in this topic and getting me to put my thoughts in order about it. I am also indebted to the people who attended my seminar—and who helped clarify my thinking— in the lecture series on "The Internet and Its Impacts on Society" at the university. I am also grateful to the Russell Sage Foundation and the Carnegie Foundation for a grant under the Russell Sage program on the Social Dimensions of Inequality (see http://www. russellsage.org/programs/proj_reviews/social-inequality.htm).

Thanks also go to Andrew Kohut of the Pew Research Center for the People and the Press for providing me with the data from the technology survey and to the Inter-University Consortium for Political and Social Research, which made data from the 1996 American National Election Study available and especially to Lee Rainie of the Pew Internet and American Life Survey for making the 2000 and 2003 Pew surveys available (and for being a great resource more generally). None of these kind folks are responsible for my interpretations. And I am grateful to the General Research Board of the University of Maryland–College Park for a Distinguished University Research Fellowship that facilitated this research.

Sources

Alexis de Tocqueville, *Democracy in America,* vol. 2, translated by Henry Reeve (New York: Alfred A. Knopf, 1945) and originally published in 1840; Robert D. Putnam, *Making Democracy Work: Civic Traditions in Modern Italy* (Princeton: Princeton Univ. Press, 1993); Robert D. Putnam, *Bowling Alone* (New York: Simon and Schuster, 2000); R. E. Kraut, W. Scherlis, M. Patterson, S. Kiesler, and T. Mukhopadhyay, "Social Impact of the Internet: What Does It Mean?" *Communications of the ACM* , vol. 41 (1998); Norman H. Nie and Lutz Erbring, "Internet and Society: A Preliminary Report," Stanford

Institute for the Quantitative Study of Society, Stanford University, 2000; "The Web's Dark Side," in *US News and World Report* (August 28, 2000); M. Hauben and R. Hauben, *Netizens* (Los Alamitos, CA: IEEE Computer Society Press, 1997); Sidney Verba, Kay Lehman Schlozman, and Henry Brady, *Voice and Equality: Civic Voluntarism in American Politics* (Cambridge: Harvard Univ. Press, 1995); Eric M. Uslaner, *The Moral Foundations of Trust* (New York: Cambridge Univ. Press, 2002) and also: "Trust, Civic Engagement, and the Internet," *Political Communication,* vol. 21; Jenny Preece, "Empathic Communities: Balancing Emotional and Factual Communication," *Interacting with Computers,* vol. 12 (1999). The technique of ordered probit analysis is analogous to multiple regression when the dependent variables (what I wish to explain) are categorical rather than continuous. I use other variables to ensure that the relationships between Internet usage, on the one hand, and trust and sociability, on the other hand, are not spurious. The other variables are: age, gender, being a student, family income, owning your own home, being self-employed, being single, having no religion, how much time you watch television each day, how often you read a newspaper, whether you trust the federal government, and whether you believe that the Internet helps keep people in touch with one another. For a discussion that neither the Internet nor television remakes people's personalities, see: Eric M. Uslaner, "Social Capital, Television, and the 'Mean World': Trust, Optimism, and Civic Participation," *Political Psychology,* vol. 19 (September, 1998); for a discussion of trust and community, see: James E. Katz and Phillip Aspden, "Social and Public Policy Internet Research: Goals and Achievements," http://www.communitytechnology.org/aspden/aspden_talk.html (1998), accessed December 30, 1999, and Kevin A. Hill and John E. Hughes, "Computer-Mediated Political Communication: The USENET and Political Communities," *Political Communication,* vol. 14 (1997), and also Patricia Wallace, *The Psychology of the Internet* (New York: Cambridge Univ. Press, 1999). To add to the point that surfing the Internet will not turn a misanthrope into a truster, one must also be mindful that other independent variables in the analysis are: age, whether you own your own home, family income, education, whether you say that you are a "born again" or Evangelical Christian, whether you are employed, how often you call friends, and how often you visit your family. Only education is statistically significant in the model. Ideally, I should estimate a simultaneous equation model to test for the possible reciprocal effects of trust and Internet usage. However, these results are so weak that such modeling would not yield different conclusions.

Table 6-1. What Shapes Internet Use? Findings from Survey of the General Public from the Pew Research Center for the People and the Press 1998

Types of Internet Use Effects of Trust and Sociability

Use e-mail Get health information Get business information Get sports news Get stock quotes Give your views online Buy goods online	Interpersonal trust generally doesn't matter for most types of computer usage. People who use e-mail are more likely to trust others and people who buy goods online are slightly more trusting. There is little evidence that simply going online creates or destroys communities. Most relationships with trust are weak and there are no significant relationships with any form of traditional social networks.
How much time use computer How much time online yesterday How many times went online yesterday Believe you go online too much	People who go online a lot are NOT more likely to be misanthropes, and they have strong social bonds. They have good social support networks and are more likely to have visited family.
Visit online chat rooms Make new friends online	People who visit chat rooms or who make new friends online are NOT the likely foundations of a new civil society. They are no more likely than others to have strong social support networks or to have visited family or called friends yesterday. They are *less* likely to trust other people.
Worry about online privacy Worry about security of medical records Worry might download virus	People who worry about their privacy or security on the Internet are far less trusting than people who aren't so worried. This reflects the general idea of trust as an optimistic worldview, however, rather than anything specific to the Internet.

The Cosmopolitan Project: Does the Internet Have a Global Public Face?

Thomas C. Hilde

It is commonly said that a principal meaning of globalization is that the world is "becoming smaller," that "distances are collapsing," or that "we are all interconnected." In conjunction with economic globalization, conventional wisdom says that new technologies, increasingly widespread access to diverse kinds of information, news, and means of communication are drawing human beings "closer together." Regardless of whether or not there is any concrete truth to these metaphors, the Internet is at the center of a constellation of factors that comprises the sentiment.

At the time of this writing, the first round of the United Nations World Summit on the Information Society has concluded in Geneva with the release of its *Draft Declaration on Principles* and its *Draft Plan of Action*. The *Draft* calls for "digital solidarity, both at the national and international levels." While the details are too extensive to examine fully here, the *Draft* declares the participants'

> ... common desire and commitment to build a people-centered, inclusive and development-oriented Information Society, where everyone can create, access, utilize and share information and knowledge, enabling individuals, communities and peoples to achieve their full potential in promoting their sustainable development and improving their quality of life.

One of the central goals of the Summit is the elimination of barriers of *access* to information and communications technologies (ICTs), particularly for the poor. Other important goals are the development of skills needed for such access, and the implementation of means by which the "Information Society" could include all the world's peoples while enabling them to retain their cultural heritage. At the same time, civil society groups, concerned that the agreement mainly represents the views of governments and businesses, are exerting pressure on the Summit leaders. These groups seek not only greater assistance to poor countries, but they also insist that human rights, the preservation of local culture, knowledge, and linguistic diversity should be central elements in the development of the Internet. Just as the advantages and disadvantages of globalization are unequally distributed, so are the benefits of the Internet.

Combining such grand visions with an unlimited variety of local concerns makes it difficult to know where to start. This inclusive "cosmopolitan" project—complex and idealistic as it is—is nevertheless precisely the central issue regarding the Internet, civic life, and civil society in the age of *"felt* interconnectedness." It is unclear whether diverse cultural forms of human communication can be placed at the forefront of globalization, preventing economic globalization from shaping the communicative sphere for us. Perhaps economic globalization will exert a great influence on the communicative sphere, since ICTs are both its product and facilitator.

Resolving the issues raised by the United Nations *Declaration* is not only beyond the scope of this paper, it is beyond the scope of anyone at this point. The technologies are still new and undergoing development in a variety of directions, and their social effects are as yet largely conjectural. I remain skeptical of many of the claims of both the promise and the perils of the Internet. Relying on recent examples to look for guidance, I discuss below some key features in thinking through the complex of community, cosmopolis, and ICTs. One slightly simpler question that I can begin with is this: if we grant communitarian concerns about the Internet, can we nonetheless see it as entering into the service of a cosmopolitanism sensitive to communal concerns?

Technologies

The twentieth-century philosophical debates about technology involved the degree to which technologies interact *neutrally* with human values imported from beyond technological uses, or whether modern technologies have come to be *constitu* 116

human values and relationships. This polar fr

logical and ethical question of technology ha

residue of techno-suspicion remains, especially in

ian thought. Yet, the Internet is especially complex as techni

because of its relative interactivity. It is not possible to speak of the Internet as one monolithic entity—this would be similar to speaking about "society" or "economy" without discerning classes, vocations, families, commercial enterprise, executive agencies, civic organizations, public fora, the functioning of various institutions, environment, and so on. Despite or perhaps because of its military beginnings, the shape of the Internet has been dominated largely by American-led commercial enterprise, large and small, in the service of *economic* globalization (and more specifically, the doctrine of "free trade"). Nonetheless, one can also find on the Internet various creative outposts, idiosyncratic corners, and even sources of real political influence.

The philosopher Andrew Feenberg reminds us that "the computer was not destined by some inner techno-logic to serve as a communications medium . . . the major networks, such as the French Teletel and the Internet were originally conceived by technocrats and engineers as instruments for the distribution of data." But "in the course of the implantation of these networks, users appropriated them for unintended purposes and converted them into communications media." As a technology, the Internet is unique in this respect: even if many users in fact live passive Internet lives, the medium itself is potentially—and often actually—interactive and, at this point, malleable enough to serve human needs that have their origins in the offline world. In the case of the Internet, the technology has been transformed into a dating service and a supplier of endless amounts of pornography, but it also addresses a steady flow of other types of concerns and needs brought to the technology from the offline world.

Consider also the recent ascendance of the blog (short for "weblog"). Blogging software enables users either to publish online diaries or to engage in interactive conversations on the Internet. Importantly, the software does not require a background in computer programming to set up or use, and has thus proliferated on the Internet—an estimated half a million blog sites at present since its introduction in the mid-1990s. The technology has become especially important in the political arena. Blogs usually have running com-

ntary of political events and ideas with hyperlinks to relevant
exts, other similar blogs, contrary positions, and other resources. The
sites often function as much better sources of information and analysis than anything found in American mass media or often even of the
better American newspapers. One campaign in the 2003–2004
American presidential campaign season has made particularly effective use of blogs in mobilizing activists, in fund-raising, and in the
broad-based development of ideas that sustain and expand the campaign. Members of Howard Dean's campaign firmly believe they are
engaged in participatory democracy, and to a large extent this can be
seen structurally in the decentralized, functional aspects of the campaign.

Other examples suggest that the Internet is a supplemental and
powerful tool in mobilizing and reinvigorating political activism with
real effects beyond the world of the Internet. Much of the international human rights regime, the antiwar movement, and the environmental movement, among many others, have bolstered their development
by using the Internet to augment the traditional routes of governmental and intergovernmental power and agreements. James
Rosenau has suggested that the "weblike explosion of organizations
has occurred in territorial space as well as cyberspace, but the opening up of the latter has served as a primary stimulus to associational
proliferation in the former." Much of the force of such civil society
organizations has derived from their ability to use the Internet as an
organizational tool. And, while not wielding institutionalized political power, much of their influence has come through the ability to
petition, to open different types of dialogue, and to shame or embarrass those who do wield political power when such power functions
contrary to the wishes or needs of people. Robert Goodin remarks that
"those may seem paltry powers. But before dismissing them entirely,
recall that that is the principal mechanism by which business gets
done among states themselves . . . the swaggering of realpolitik theo-
reticians notwithstanding." I would add that, apart from the internal
structures of such organizations, their influence is serving to create,
propagate, or disseminate the conditions (such as the human rights
discourse) that may make a more diverse and inclusive Internet
sphere possible in the future.

One can easily imagine the broadened base of access promoted by
the UN and others as leading not only to a proliferation of views, dialogue, and information, but also a proliferation of new software

developed out of specific contextualized needs in widely varying locales. One can also easily imagine the proliferation of more fluff, more idiosyncratic sites of self-dialogue, more shopping, more ingenious ways to extract people's credit card numbers and other private information. Furthermore, as Peter Levine very helpfully discusses in his contribution to this volume, the Internet may serve to exacerbate features that are already problematic in the broader society (such as diminished equity, weakened social bonds, threats to public deliberation and to privacy). The UN *Declaration* speaks to some of these problems, some of which likely have easier solutions (privacy) than others (equity). Answering whether the Internet necessarily exacerbates these problems requires that we look at which kinds of culture have dominated the shape of the Internet to this point (and will for the foreseeable future). The negative characteristics cited are mirrored in that broader culture and existed long before the creation of the Internet. There also exists the possibility that greater global access could lead to greater diversity of uses and communication in the Internet and, even more idealistically, greater solidarity in the world beyond the Internet.

Community

A preliminary way to define community is to say that community comprises shared beliefs, values, and modes of valuation, along with commitments, activities, and rites that are considered good by those who participate in them. A broad but important set of questions examines whether or not the Internet promotes community or public "space." One fear is that, just as ICTs function by disassembling messages into bits of information, transferring the bits of data at high speed, and reassembling them at the receiving end, globalization *takes apart* traditional modes of human interaction and reassembles them. Put differently, the question is whether the Internet strengthens or dissolves community, whether it brings otherwise isolated people together in meaningful ways, whether Internet groups' low thresholds of entry and exit encourage lack of commitment, whether it invigorates or atomizes public life, whether it promotes or sustains the deliberative processes integral to healthy civic life, and so on. Clearly, electronic communication and interaction are no substitute for face-to-face communication and interaction. The issue obviously turns on how one conceptualizes community from the outset. This may run the gamut from a thin version of communities as temporary, voluntary "communities of interest" to much thicker notions of community defined by an oppressive lack of choice or, for example, as represented in the security fetish of some modern societies. At issue is not, for example, philosopher Charles Peirce's model of a truth-seeking scientific community of inquirers, because one may assuredly argue that the Internet facilitates the processes and interchanges of this kind of community as it is approximated in practice. The issue is also comparatively a matter of placed community, what William Galston's example of the Portuguese public square points up in the present volume—the same public interaction (and spaces designed for it or created through it) can be found throughout Latin America, in much of Africa, Europe, and parts of Asia, but increasingly less so in the United States unless commercialized and high security. We need to ask ourselves continually why this phenomenon is or should be the case in the United States.

A central concern appears to be what the American philosopher, Josiah Royce, nearly a century ago called the "detached individual":

> the individualism of the man who belongs to no community which he loves and to which he can devote himself with all his heart, and his soul, and his mind, and his strength . . . mere detachment, mere self-will, can never be satisfied with itself, can never win its goal. What saves us on any level of human social life is union.

Insofar as the cosmopolitan is a "citizen of the world" in the sense of being attached to no place and no one, the detached individual just *is* the cosmopolitan.

The evidence, anecdotal as it largely is at this point in the Internet's history, seems to lead toward the negative answer to the above set of questions. Among the reasons given for the conjecture that the Internet weakens or fragments community and public life are that participants are isolated, Internet groups are allowed easy exit and exhibit little commitment, and one typically sees only temporary social ties and understandings.

On the other hand, an important recent study of a "wired community" near Toronto by two MIT and University of Toronto researchers, Keith Hampton and Barry Wellman, suggests that Internet users may actually be *more* inclined to human neighborhood interaction outside of time spent in front of the computer compared to those who are less Internet-active. While, again, any Internet study should be taken with some skepticism, this study examined not only "life online," but the broader range of Internet users' personal and technologically mediated human contacts. This seems a crucial issue in any such study—whether Internet use comes to be a substitute for other offline activities and ideas or whether it augments offline activities and ideas. The authors argue that

> Online social ties are not a distinct social system, separate and cut off from existing foci of activity and existing social network members. Rather, the Internet affects community as one form of communication among many, whose use and implications are intertwined.

They further argue that the Internet has a number of advantages over other forms of communication, including "its ability to facilitate neighborhood based interactions, specifically the asynchronous, broadcast ability of e-mail." The strong implication here—that the Internet may strengthen local community ties more generally—is difficult to accept, given the local nature of the research. But one may nevertheless at least conclude the weak implication from the study that impediments to local community are more a function of other features of modern life than they are of online life.

On communitarian grounds, one can find weaknesses to the view that the Internet serves to strengthen community in a substantive way. One can also be concerned about what this means for our human future given the increasingly pervasive role of the Internet in various facets of human lives. This communitarian type of critique is at least agnostic regarding the Internet when not in advocacy of its nonuse. But one wonders what to do with the stronger form of this critique. The Internet and ICTs have an air of inevitability about them. Is there a communitarian option? It is not clear what this would be, beyond either overly aggressive political action or individuals or tight-knit groups opting out. Only the opt-out option is feasible and, indeed, desirable for some. It appears that what remain are a communitarian agnosticism and a cautionary note well-taken regarding ICT development and implementation and regarding offline life. But the Hampton and Wellman study, if representative, seems to show that the problem has been framed in a misleading way. The study confirms that the problems of dissolution for community predate the existence of the Internet and may be found in other activities of contemporary postindustrial life. It suggests at the very least that the Internet does not necessarily accelerate or exacerbate these problems.

Global Cosmopolitanism

Detachment, however, is equally problematic at the level of communities and intercommunal relationships. The preeminent philosopher of democratic community, John Dewey, insisted that the quality of the community depended not only on "many interests consciously communicated and shared," but also on "varied and free points of contact with other modes of association." The former condition requires novelty and equity, among other imperatives. The latter condition, the one I am most concerned with here, requires interaction with other groups. As Dewey wrote in a discussion of democratic community,

> It is a commonplace that an alert and expanding mental life depends upon an enlarging range of contact with the physical environment. But the principle applies even more significantly to the field where we are apt to ignore it—the social sphere.

For his part, the religious communitarian and internationalist Royce maintained the importance of encouraging the young to go out of the community (or "province") and learn from others in order to return with "what they thus acquire for the furtherance of the life of their own community." Many "points of contact" is empty unless this entails the existence of various options as well as openness to transformation on the part of individuals and groups. It resists the vision of an archipelago of isolated communities. Minimally, this notion of communities requires curiosity as well as practical outlets for the satisfaction of curiosity.

But we can go farther. Full public life is increasingly global in cause and consequence. To use an apt cliché: the local is global. The selfhood of individuals is increasingly defined in terms beyond tradition, church, family, vocation, and neighborhood, though these all remain in some form. Communities have always had boundaries permeable to ideas and "outsiders"; they are much more so in the "global" age. And some of the most pressing problems individuals, communities, and nations face are transnational in nature (e.g., environmental problems and risks, disease, terrorism and other aggression, human rights). Mass media and ICTs impact the lives of a growing number of people, if not most, worldwide. Migration and global travel—not new phenomena—grow through necessity and desire. Human experience is a history of stasis and security, but it is also a history of travel and insecurity. When it is not of the Club Med variety, replicating conditions or ideals of comfort from home, travel may provoke and transform. We return at least slightly and maybe even radically different people or perhaps do not return at all. On the other hand, migration entails a complex overlapping and conciliation of sometimes very different, conflicting worlds of value.

These observations do not necessarily constitute a kind of cultural cosmopolitanism. They are not merely the fantasies of detached "postmodern bourgeois liberals," as often derided. They are real facets of life and represent both possibilities for and foreclosures of diverse cultural ties. Consider, for example, Helena Norberg-Hodge's studies of the remote region of Ladakh in the Indian Himalayas and Tibetan Plateau. She describes a former socially and environmentally sustainable, and peaceful, traditional culture reshaped during the past thirty years by the introduction of tourism, Western mass media, and Western-style education based in "universal knowledge." Norberg-Hodge maintains that this restructuring of Ladakhi society has led not only to an uprooting of ideas and practices from their context, but to a society of shame in which younger generations compare themselves negatively to their televised Western counterparts and find themselves to be poor and uneducated. The effects have been ruinous for Ladakhi culture—from an increase in acquisitiveness over cooperation, to unsustainable consumption practices, to an increase in ethnic violence as different groups compete for limited resources. Norberg-Hodge ascribes these changes to the broader notion of "globalization." Perhaps one of the most tragic aspects of such examples is that just as a group is accepting and adapting to a way of life imported from elsewhere, that way of life is undergoing its own intense criticism of itself as unsustainable. The Ladakh example (and an endless number could be cited) points up the viruslike nature of a *particular kind* of Western culture and asymmetrical cultural contact. Such cases provide an admonition, for both the sake of us and others, against uncritically embracing the free-flow of cultural artifacts. It suggests responsibilities pulling in a number of directions, as the consequences of certain lifestyles impede upon those of others.

Considerations such as those outlined above are among the global cultural issues that have partially driven a resurgence in both communitarian and cosmopolitan thought, a parting of the ways in relation to global issues faced by everyone. Cosmopolitans "hold to a vision that accepts, even celebrates, the diversity of social and political systems in the world, taking pleasure in the existence and the products of peoples and places other than our homes . . . display concern for our fellow humans without demanding of them that they be or become like ourselves." In theoretical terms, moral and political cosmopolitanism are hotly debated in philosophy and political thought. Although there exists a diverse and growing range of views within each of these categories, moral cosmopolitanism generally constitu. sets of arguments for obligations to aid human beings as human beings apart from the boundaries of region or nation. It inclu es foreigners or strangers as candidates for moral consideration and obligation rather than only those in more intimate relations of community. Political cosmopolitanism generally insists on the view that political institutions should map onto and reflect these moral duties, especially in response to problems that cross borders or as the counterpart to economic globalization. Such institutions could range from "world government" to interactively layered local, regional, and global institutions.

In contrast to this approach, I want to propose that what is needed is something along the lines of an *epistemic cosmopolitanism* that does some work toward reconciling the disjunctive communitarian and cosmopolitan responses to globalization (and the role of ICTs). Like communitarian views, epistemic cosmopolitanism accepts and defends the "thickness" of values and beliefs embedded in particular contexts. Any inquiry in which humans engage is attached to particular contexts of belief, history, and environment. There is no discernible moral or political viewpoint beyond such contexts that could legitimately represent all concerns, beliefs, and values of all communities. But, as a form of cosmopolitanism, epistemic cosmopolitanism treats those contexts empirically as increasingly global. It takes tradition seriously. It also takes seriously the possibilities of curiosity and transformation by indicating that our individual and communal knowing, valuing, and believing draws upon and contributes to an expanded and globalizing range of ideas, beliefs, practices, events, and traditions. It does so in such a way that problems we individually and collectively face may, at times, be tackled best through changing the conceptions of community or individual with which we start. In other words, it takes as its starting point the basic idea that communities and individuals are not fixed but evolving entities. Better or worse forms of both are a function of whether those forms serve toward resolving real, practical problems. Epistemic cosmopolitanism expresses the fallibility and possible revision of the positions brought to the table in resolving practical problems. It celebrates not the detached "citizen of the world" belonging to no place and no one, but contextualized peoples and communities whose "memberships" increasingly stretch beyond traditional notions of membership. The idea is that this then entails a broader variety of practical means and ends for thinking through problems we face collectively. Even if participants in collective action are not all led to one overarching principled view of the way things should be, they are at least aware of the practical constraints and possibilities of their views.

If the public is shaped less as a congealing of collective identities for the sake of shoring up identity, but more as a collective response to the problems human beings face, then we should be able to speak of the public itself as globalizing. The question then involves the shape in which globalized society takes. This is precisely the difficulty to which the United Nations *Declaration* responds.

Conclusion

We ought not to be overly sanguine about the prospects of the Internet, especially since its present form and content are still largely based on a particular culture's activities posing as universal culture. But, I have been suggesting, this need not necessarily be the case, and the technologies involved as well as the informational and communicative content are rapidly changing as more people in more places are online. Clearly, issues of equity and a host of other problems regarding the Internet still require attention and resolution. It is not clear, however, that this resolution can be found without resolving them first in our broader societies and between societies. The tendency to substitute online detachment for affective, embodied interaction with other human beings or intensified "communities" of like-minded individuals sharing their fears and fantasies in isolated and antagonistic groups will win out only to the extent that societies allow other avenues of communication to shut down, such as public space. But there seems to me no reason to see the Internet as inherently fated to shut down dialogue and deliberation, and to reinforce *bad* habits of community. Rather, I find persuasive indications that creative combinations of communal life online and communal life offline are only as good as the variety of features of local, national, and global society allow.

This chapter was based on an earlier work in *Philosophy & Public Policy Quarterly,* volume 24, winter/spring 2004.

Sources

United Nations, *Draft Declaration of Principles,* World Summit on the Information Society (December 9, 2003) Document WSIS/PC-3/DT/6(Rev 3)-E; for a comprehensive review of twentieth-century philosophical debates about the degree to which technologies interact with human values, see Carl Mitcham, *Thinking Through Technology* (Chicago: Univ. of Chicago Press, 1994); Andrew Feenberg, *Questioning Technology* (London: Routledge, 1999). For a discussion of how the Howard Dean campaign has made effective use of blogs, see Helen Shapiro, "The Dean Connection," *New York Times Magazine* (December 7, 2003); James Rosenau, *Distant Proximities* (Princeton: Princeton Univ. Press, 2003); Robert Goodin, "Globalizing Justice," in *Taming Globalization,* edited by David Held and Mathias Koenig-Archibugi (Cambridge: Polity Press, 2003). For discussions of whether the Internet strengthens or dissolves community, see Uslaner, Galston, and Levine's articles in this present volume. For a discussion of notions of community, see Zygmunt Bauman, *Community: Seeking Safety in an Insecure World* (Cambridge: Polity Press, 2001); Charles S. Peirce, "Some Consequences of Four Incapacities," originally published in 1868, and found in *The Essential Peirce,* edited by Nathan Houser and Christian Kloesel (Bloomington: Indiana Univ. Press, 1992). The importance of certain forms of physical space for a rich public life cannot be underestimated. The American tendency to rely on the market for even the physical ordering of lived environments means that possibilities for public life in physical space are sometimes hit upon only accidentally. For broader discussions of this tension regarding public space, see Jane Jacobs' classic *The Death and Life of American Cities* (New York: Vintage, 1961), *Variations on a Theme Park* (New York: Hill and Wang, 1994), edited by Michael Sorkin, and James Howard Kunstler, *The City in Mind* (New York: Free Press, 2003). Josiah Royce, "The Hope of the Great Community," originally published in 1916, and found in *The Basic Writings of Josiah Royce, Volume 2,* edited by John J. McDermott (Chicago: Univ. of Chicago Press, 1969); Keith Hampton and Barry Wellman, "Neighboring in Netville: How the Internet Supports Community and Social Capital in a Wired Suburb," in *City and Community* (vols. 2 & 3, Fall 2003); see also www.chass.utoronto.ca/~wellman/publications/index.htm. John Dewey, *Democracy and Education* (New York: Free Press, 1916); Josiah Royce, "Provincialism," which originally appeared in 1908, in volume 2, cited above; for further discussion, also see Thomas C. Hilde, "Provincialism, Displacement, and Royce's Idea of Community," in

The Agrarian Roots of Pragmatism, edited by Paul B. Thompson and Thomas C. Hilde (Nashville, TN: Vanderbilt Univ. Press, 2000). The expression "postmodern bourgeois liberalism" is Richard Rorty's; see his article of the same term, in his work *Objectivity, Relativism, and Truth* (Cambridge: Cambridge Univ. Press, 1991). Helena Norberg-Hodge, "The Pressure to Modernize and Globalize," in *The Case Against the Global Economy,* edited by Jerry Mander and Edward Goldsmith (San Francisco: Sierra Club Books, 1996); see also her earlier book, *Ancient Futures: Learning from Ladakh* (San Francisco: Sierra Club Books, 1991). The contention that cosmopolitans accept diversity without demanding that others themselves become cosmopolitans is made by K. Anthony Appiah, "Citizens of the World," in *Globalizing Rights,* edited by Matthew J. Gibney (Oxford: Oxford Univ. Press, 2003). A more detailed discussion of these views, as well as the array of anticosmopolitan arguments, is beyond the scope of this chapter. For an interesting overview of some of the historical roots of cosmopolitanism, see Thomas J. Schlereth, *The Cosmopolitan Ideal in Enlightenment Thought* (Notre Dame: Notre Dame Univ. Press, 1977). Among the numerous contemporary examples of cosmopolitan works, see Martha Nussbaum, *For Love of Country?* (Boston: Beacon Press, 2002); Thomas Pogge, *World Poverty and Human Rights* (Cambridge: Polity Press, 2002); David Held, *Democracy and the Global Order: From the Modern State to Cosmopolitan Governance* (Cambridge: Polity Press, 1995); Onora O'Neill, *Bounds of Justice* (Cambridge: Cambridge Univ. Press, 2000); Peter Singer, *One World: The Ethics of Globalization* (New Haven: Yale Univ. Press, 2002). For a nuanced critique of cosmopolitanism, see the essays by Will Kymlicka in his *Politics in the Vernacular* (Oxford: Oxford Univ. Press, 2001).

Index

About the Editor and Contributors

William A. Galston is director of the Institute for Philosophy and Public Policy, Saul I. Stern Professor of Civic Engagement at the School of Public Affairs at the University of Maryland, and director of the Center for Information & Research on Civic Learning & Engagement (CIRCLE). He is a political theorist who both studies and participates in American politics and domestic policy. He was deputy assistant to the president for Domestic Policy, 1993–1995, and executive director of the National Commission on Civic Renewal, 1996–1999. Galston served as a founding member of the Board of the National Campaign to Prevent Teen Pregnancy and as chair of the campaign's task force on religion and public values. He is the author of five books and nearly one hundred articles in moral and political theory, American politics, and public policy. His publications include *Liberal Purposes* (Cambridge, 1991) and *Liberal Pluralism* (Cambridge, 2002).

Verna V. Gehring is editor at the Institute for Philosophy and Public Policy at the School of Public Affairs, University of Maryland. She is a philosopher broadly interested in the obligations of state and citizen and the various accounts of civil society. In addition to her work on the seventeenth-century political philosopher Thomas Hobbes and his enduring influence, Gehring's interest is applied to such contemporary matters as the state lottery, nuclear proliferation, computer hackers, baseball scandals, and the social harms caused by imposters. She is editor in chief of *Philosophy & Public Policy Quarterly,* coeditor (with William A. Galston) of *Philosophical Dimensions of Public Policy* (2002), and editor of *War after September 11* (2002) and *Genetic Prospects: Essays on Biotechnology, Ethics, and Public Policy* (2003).

Thomas C. Hilde is visiting assistant professor in the School of Public Affairs at the University of Maryland. Before coming to MSPA, he taught environmental thought at New York University where he was also acting director of the Environmental Conservation Program and of the Applied Philosophy Group. Hilde studies social and political philosophy and ethics. He is especially interested in applied issues regarding international development, the environment, art, policy and politics. He coedited (with Paul B. Thompson) *The Agrarian Roots of Pragmatism* (2000), and is editor of the forthcoming *Pragmatism and Globalism,* cotranslator of *Stalinism and Nazism: History and Memory Compared* (2004), and author of a forthcoming volume on globalization.

Lucas D. Introna is reader in Organization, Technology, and Ethics at the Lancaster University Management School, which he joined in September 2000. Prior to this appointment, he lectured in Information Systems and Political Science at the London School of Economics. He is also visiting professor of Information Systems at the University of Pretoria. His research interest is the social dimensions of information technology and its consequences for society. In particular he is concerned with the way information technology transforms and mediates social interaction. Among numerous professional memberships, Introna is founding coeditor of *Ethics and Information Technology,* a founding member of the International Society for Ethics and Information Technology (INSEIT), a member of the editorial board of *Philosophy in the Contemporary World,* associate editor of *Information Technology & People,* and coeditor of *Ethics and Information Technology.* His most recent work includes *Management, Information and Power* (Macmillan, 1997). His various academic papers treat a variety of topics, such as theories of information, information technology and ethics, autopoiesis and social systems, and virtual organizations. His current research interests include the ethics of mediated intersubjectivity, the phenomenology of information technology, and cooperative work in virtual environments.

Peter Levine (www.peterlevine.ws) is deputy director of CIRCLE, The Center for Information and Research on Civic Learning and

Engagement (www.civicyouth.org). CIRCLE conducts and funds research on young people's civic education and participation. Levine is also a research scholar at the Institute for Philosophy and Public Policy in the University of Maryland's School of Public Affairs. From 1991 until 1993, he was a research associate at Common Cause, helping that organization to lobby for campaign finance reform and government ethics. In the late 1990s, he was deputy director of the National Commission on Civic Renewal, chaired by Senator Sam Nunn and William Bennett. Levine is also an associate for the Charles Kettering Foundation. He is a cofounder of the Deliberative Democracy Consortium (www.deliberative-democracy.net). Levine is the author of four books. He also co-organized the writing of *The Civic Mission of Schools*, a report released by Carnegie Corporation of New York and CIRCLE in 2003 (www.civicmissionofschools.org). In Prince George's County, Maryland, Levine is working with high school students to create an "Information Commons" (see www.princegeorges.org). This is an association devoted to building a state-of-the-art Web site with asset maps, news articles, structured deliberations, and other public goods.

Helen Nissenbaum is associate professor in the Department of Culture and Communication and a senior fellow of the Information Law Institute, New York University. She specializes in social, ethical, and political dimensions of information technology. Her published works on privacy, property rights, electronic publication, accountability, the use of computers in education, and values embodied in computer systems have appeared in scholarly journals of philosophy, applied ethics, law, and computer science. She is author of *Emotion and Focus* (University of Chicago Press), coeditor (with D. J. Johnson), *Computers, Ethics and Social Values* (Prentice-Hall), and a founding coeditor of the journal *Ethics and Information Technology* (Kluwer Academic Press). Grants from the National Science Foundation and Ford Foundation have supported her research, and she has served on committees of the National Academy of Sciences, National Science Foundation, UNESCO, AAAS, and the ACM. Before joining NYU, Nissenbaum was a member of the School of Social Science, Institute for Advanced Study, associate director of Princeton University Center for Human Values, and postdoctoral fellow at the Center for the Study of Language and Information, Stanford University. She earned a B.A. (Honors) from the University of Witwatersand, Johannesburg and a Ph.D. in philosophy from Stanford University.

Eric M. Uslaner is professor of Government and Politics at the University of Maryland, College Park, where he has taught since 1975. He has written seven books, including *The Moral Foundations of Trust* (Cambridge University Press, 2002), *The Decline of Comity in Congress* (University of Michigan Press, 1993), and *The Movers and the Shirkers: Representatives and Ideologues in the Senate* (University of Michigan Press, 1999), and over fifty articles. Uslaner's edited books include *Social Capital and Participation in Everyday Life* and *Social Capital and the Transition to Democracy* (both published by Routledge). He is frequently quoted in the national press, including the *Washington Post* and the *New York Times,* and has also been a contributor to the *Wall Street Journal.* Professor Uslaner has testified before committees in the United States Congress. He has appeared on television in the United States, Mexico, and Japan. He has lectured widely in the United States, Canada, Latin America, Europe, Israel, and Asia and delivered the keynote lecture at the International Conference on Social Capital, Economic and Research Institute of the Cabinet Office, Government of Japan, Tokyo, Japan, March 25, 2003. In 1981–82 he was Fulbright Professor of American Studies and Political Science at the Hebrew University, Jerusalem, Israel. In 1997–98 he was named Distinguished University Research Fellow, University of Maryland. In 2000 he won the Mentor of the Year Award from the Southern Regional Education Board. Currently, Uslaner is conducting research on the linkage between trust, inequality, and civic engagement in the United States (with a grant from the Russell Sage Foundation), and (with a grant from the Starr Foundation) research on "Civil Society and Development on the Black Sea: Social Involvement in Romania and the Republic of Moldova."

Robert Wachbroit is research scholar at the Institute for Philosophy and Public Policy, at the School of Public Policy, University of Maryland. He is also adjunct associate professor of OB/GYN in the University's School of Medicine. He has written articles in the areas of philosophy of science, philosophy of medicine, and medical ethics, including articles on the principles of disease classification, the challenges of genetic testing and diagnosis, and the problem inherent in human cloning and genetic enhancements. He has also written about the role of expertise in public deliberations and on the impact of the Internet on civil society. He is co-editor (with David Wasserman) of *Genetics and Criminal Behavior* (2001) and (with David Wasserman and Jerome Bickenbach) *Quality of Life and Human Difference: Genetic Testing, Health-Care, and Disability* (Cambridge University Press, forthcoming).